SAVE THE MALES

Why Men Are Mistreated, Misdiagnosed and Misunderstood.

by

KENNETH WETCHER, M.D.,
ART BARKER, M.A.
AND
F. REX MCCAUGHTRY, M.S.W.

This book is not intended to replace personal medical care and/or professional supervision; there is no substitute for the experience and information that your doctor or mental health professional can provide. Rather, it is our hope that this book will provide additional information to help people understand the changing role of men and the emotional and psychiatric problems that can evolve.

Proper treatment should always be tailored to the individual. If you read something in this book that seems to conflict with your doctor or mental health professional's instructions, contact him/her. There may be sound reasons for recommending treatment that may differ from the information presented in this book.

If you have any questions about any treatment in this book, please consult your doctor or mental health care professional.

In addition, the names and cases used in this book do not represent actual people, but are composite cases drawn from several sources.

All rights reserved
Copyright © 1991 The PIA Press

No part of this book may be reproduced or transmitted
in any form or by any means, electronic or mechanical,
including photocopying, recording, or by any information
storage and retrieval system, without permission in writing from
the publisher.
For information write:
Psychiatric Institutes of America,
part of the National Medical Enterprises Specialty Hospital Group.
1010 Wisconsin Ave. NW
Washington, D.C. 20007

Other Books Available

The Good News About Depression, by Mark S. Gold, M.D.
The Good News About Panic, Anxiety and Phobias, by Mark S. Gold, M.D.
Sixty Ways to Make Stress Work For You, by Andrew E. Slaby, M.D., Ph.D., M.P.H.
Guide To The New Medicines Of The Mind, by Irl Extein, M.D., Larry S. Kirstein, M.D., and Peter Herridge, M.D.
The Facts About Drugs and Alcohol, 3rd edition, by Mark S. Gold, M.D.
Get Smart About Weight Control, by Phillip M. Sinaikin, M.D.
High Times/Low Times: The Many Faces of Adolescent Depression, by John E. Meeks, M.D.
On the Edge: The Love/Hate World of the Borderline Personality, by Neil D. Price, M.D.
Overcoming Insomnia, by Donald R. Sweeney, M.D., Ph.D.
Light Up Your Blues: Understanding and Overcoming Seasonal Affective Disorders, by Robert N. Moreines, M.D.
A Parent's Guide to Common and Uncommon School Problems, by David A. Gross, M.D. and Irl L. Extein, M.D.
Psychiatric Skeletons: Tracing the Legacy of Mental Illness In the Family, by Steven D. Targum, M.D.
Life On A Roller Coaster: Coping With the Ups and Downs of Mood Disorders, by Ekkehard Othmer, M.D., Ph.D., and Sieglinde C. Othmer, Ph.D.
A Consumer's Guide to Psychiatric Diagnosis, by Mark A. Gould, M.D.
Aftershock, by Andrew E. Slaby, M.D., Ph.D., M.P.H.
Kids Out of Control, by Alan M. Cohen, M.D.
A Parent's Guide To Teens and Cults, by Larry E. Dumont, M.D. and Richard I. Altesman, M.D.
The Family Contract, by Howard I. Leftin, M.D.
Family Addictions, A Guide For Surviving Alcohol and Drug Abuse, by Charles R. Norris, Jr., M.D.
Kids On the Brink: Understanding the Teen Suicide Epidemic, by David B. Bergman, M.D.
Codependency, Sexuality and Depression, by William E. Thornton, M.D.
When Self-Help Isn't Enough: Overcoming Addiction and Psychiatric Disorders, by A. Scott Winter, M.D.
No More Secrets, No More Shame: Understanding Sexual Abuse and Psychiatric Disorders, by David A. Sack, M.D.
Living with Pain by William S. Makarowski, M.D.
Living with Head Injury: A Guide for Families, by Richard C. Senelick, M.D., and Cathy E. Ryan
Kids Who Do/Kids Who Don't: A Parent's Guide To Teens and Drugs, by Lorraine Henricks, M.D.
Caught In the Crossfire: The Impact of Divorce on Young People, by Lorraine Henricks, M.D.
Teens At Risk, by Kevin Leehey, M.D.
Sit Down and Pay Attention, by Ronald Goldberg, M.D.
Save the Males, by Kenneth Wetcher, M.D., Art Barker, M.A., and F. Rex McCaughtry, M.S.W.

DEDICATION

KENNETH WETCHER, M.D.

To my loving father, Morris, who hugged and kissed me when I was a boy; who stopped hugging and kissing me when I decided it was unmanly; who let me hug and kiss him as I approached true manhood.

ART BARKER, M.A.

This book is dedicated to Martie, my wife and best friend who believes in me, to Martha and Arthur, my children who have the courage to live their beliefs, and to Carson with whom I've experienced the joy of grandfathering.

F. REX McCAUGHTRY, M.S.W.

To my grandfather, Rex Gassaway, who spent large chunks of time with me fishing, hunting, playing baseball, while at the same time teaching me intimacy, giving me identity, and building my masculine self-esteem; to my wife and soulmate, Teresa Greiner, M.D., who was wise enough to recognize our connection and bridge across forever, so we could stop the search; to Leslie Carol McCaughtry, my 3-year-old daughter, and newborn son, Ryan Scott McCaughtry, who have given meaning and purpose to my life.

CONTENTS

PART I	**The Genesis of Gender**	1
PROLOGUE	Echoes From the Talking Stick	3
CHAPTER 1	The Disposable Male	7
CHAPTER 2	The Male Stereotype	18
CHAPTER 3	The Power of Socialization	27
CHAPTER 4	Body and Soul: Physical Aspects of Maleness	39
PART II	**Men In the Danger Zone**	49
PROLOGUE	Echoes From the Talking Stick	51
CHAPTER 5	Men and Depression	53
CHAPTER 6	Men, Substance Abuse, and Addiction	67
CHAPTER 7	Men and Post-Traumatic Disorder	79
CHAPTER 8	Men and Anger, Rage and Violence	92
CHAPTER 9	Men and Workaholism, Abuse, Divorce	104
PART III	**Saving the Males**	119
PROLOGUE	Echoes From the Talking Stick	121
CHAPTER 10	Men Misunderstood, Misdiagnosed, Mistreated	123
CHAPTER 11	A New Approach	132
CHAPTER 12	Other Pathways	147
Epilogue	**A Ring Around the Moon**	161

Men's Resources 162
Sources 164
Index 166

ACKNOWLEDGMENTS

There are many individuals whom we want to thank for contributing directly and indirectly to this book. We are, first of all, grateful to Susan Smith, our mentor and the administrator at Baywood Hospital, for her courage and vision in supporting, from it's conception, the nation's first successful inpatient treatment program for men. Without her energy, this book would not have been possible.

We are grateful to John Hough, the Johnny Appleseed of men's treatment, for his contribution to our initial journey into the gender role conflicts of troubled men.

We also thank Trisha Gunn, who challenged us and on whom we tested our beliefs, and Goldie Rappaport Wetcher, whose thoughtful comments and questions helped us define our concepts.

We sincerely thank Newton Hightower, a valued friend and co-creator of the Emerging Male Weekend, who showed his clinical expertise and, most of all, allowed and encouraged us to explore our own maleness.

We are indebted to Matt Evans, a special friend and colleague, who taught and shared with us the awesome power of the Talking Stick Ceremony.

We thank Ron Schaumburg, our Merlin, who gave us his scholarship and who magically created words from ideas.

We are thankful to Nancy Shaver, our chief scribe, who kept the paperwork flowing, and the editors of PIA Press, who pulled it all together and provided the gift of creation.

We are grateful to Dar Wiginton and Vance McCaughtry for their help and feedback on fathering.

We especially thank the treatment team and nursing staff at Baywood hospital, led by Madeline West, who were open and willing to look inside themselves and grow in their treatment approach toward men and share their experiences with us. Madeline we also thank for sharing the pain and pleasure of being both the "Good and Bad Mother" of the Men's Forum at Baywood.

We want to give a special thanks to our patients, the men of the Men's Forum, inpatient and outpatient, who allowed us into their lives. They have trusted and encouraged us to continue our work to find new and better ways of treating troubled men. Through these men, we have discovered our own yearning to be a part of the brotherhood of men, the male community.

ABOUT THE AUTHORS

KENNETH WETCHER, M.D., is Medical Director of Baywood Hospital and founder and medical director of the Wetcher Clinic. Trained at Downstate Medical Center, New York, Dr. Wetcher followed with an internship and residency in Baltimore. After a tour of duty with the U.S. Air Force, he completed his residency at Baylor College of Medicine. Dr. Wetcher is a Diplomate of the American Board of Psychiatry and Neurology and a member of the American Psychiatric Association, the American Psychotherapy Association and the Texas Medical Association.

ART BARKER, L.P.C., C.A.D.A.C., is a psychotherapist with the Wetcher Clinic. Mr. Barker is the co-creator and director of the Men's Forum at the Wetcher Clinic, the Men's Forum medical liaison with Baywood Hospital, and co-creator of the "Emerging Male" weekend retreats. He is a graduate of the University of Houston, where he earned a master's degree in Family Therapy, and is a licensed professional counselor, certified alcohol and drug abuse counselor, and a certified employee assistance professional.

F. REX MCCAUGHTRY, C.S.W., A.C.P., is a psychotherapist with the Wetcher Clinic. Mr. McCaughtry is the director of clinical development at the Wetcher Clinic and director of program development at Baywood Hospital. He previously served as the first program director of the Men's Forum at the Wetcher Clinic and is actively involved in individual and group therapies involving men's issues. Prior to that he was a clinical instructor with the Baylor College of Medicine, Department of Psychiatry, and the University of Houston Graduate School of Social Work.

Part I

THE GENESIS OF GENDER

Prologue

Echoes from the Talking Stick

The men gather in the room. Some men are young, others are older. Some are black, some brown, some white. Each has doubts. Why did I decide to come here? What's going to happen? Will this really help me?

But these men have more than their doubts in common. All the men here are searching. Searching for relief from their mysterious pain. Searching for understanding of themselves and of others. Searching for a connection to these who have gathered here hoping to find new awareness and new direction in their lives.

They are searching to know what it means to be a man.

They have gathered here in a suburb of Houston to join in an *Emerging Male* weekend. These events are part of a special men's treatment program offered through Baywood Hospital and the Wetcher Clinic. The weekends are open to all men, but are especially helpful for those suffering from addiction, depression, and stress-related disorders. Our weekends are close cousins to the gatherings of men featured in a rapidly growing phenomenon often called the Men's Movement. Similar programs are *A Gathering of Men, Wild Man Weekends*, and *Warrior Training*. Within the last few years, more than 50,000 men throughout the country have participated in such weekends, where ancient rituals are used to promote male bonding, acceptance, and healing.

Here is a glimpse of how one recent Emerging Male weekend unfolded....

In the center of the room lies a collection of rhythm-makers: drums, sticks, tambourines. Nearby, perched on stands, are large drums whose burnished wood bodies shine. One of the men begins to beat a rhythm. Soon another finds an instrument and offers a variation on the pulse. Some hold back, but eventually all find a way to contribute their sound—knocking sticks together, clapping hands.

With over two dozen men participating, the rhythm becomes complex and syncopated. Some of the sounds are deep and steady; some are lighter, quicker. Each man, listening to the whole mosaic of sound, adds his own rhythmic voice, a part of the pattern but distinct in subtle ways.

The sound rises in tempo and intensity, becomes complete, and stops. The echoes fade away.

Soon afterward the men sit in a circle. So large is the gathering that it is hard to see everyone's face. In other times and other places, such a circle might have formed beside a fire or around a sacred image or totem. Tonight, however, the men sit in folding chairs in a nondescript room whose only purpose is to accommodate a coming together of men.

The leaders briefly explain the purpose of the gathering. One of the leaders then reaches into a bag and pulls out a long pouch made of deerskin. From this pouch he withdraws a stick, perhaps two feet long. The stick is different from ordinary sticks in two ways. It is encoiled by a vine that winds around its entire length. The vine coiled around the stick resembles a caduceus, the ancient symbol of medicine. This image of healing, as it will turn out, is more than just one of appearance.

The stick is also different because it contains a certain power. The leader holds the stick up for all the gathering to see. It is the Talking Stick, he explains. The stick will be passed from man to man. Each will say all that is in his heart that he wishes to reveal at that time and in that place. The stick empowers only the one holding it to speak. All the others must remain silent; if something that is said by one touches another, however, that man may respond with the simple sound of "ho," or "ah ho."

The leader holds up the stick. He looks around the room into each man's eyes and says, "Do you love yourself enough to listen with your heart to the other parts of you speak?" With that he hands it to the man sitting next to him.

As the stick makes its way around the circle, the energy within the room changes. Each man has the chance to be heard—heard perhaps more clearly than ever before in his life. Because of the ritual solemnity of the occasion, the remarks rise far above the usual level of male banter about sports and cars and women. Instead the comments, taken as a whole, reveal the collective experience—and, at times, the inner wisdom—of men.

"I'm Mike,*" says one who holds the stick. "I came to this

---

*To protect privacy, the men's names and identifying details have been changed.

weekend wondering what I'd gotten myself into. When I saw everybody drumming I thought you were all crazy. Then I realized that I was about the only one who wasn't making any noise and I thought, hell, I guess *I'm* the oddball. Then somebody handed me a tambourine and I started playing. I felt like the sound I made really contributed something. The rhythm was different because of me. I liked being part of the band we just formed, and I hope that feeling continues over the next couple of days."

One by one, the men speak....

When John receives the stick, he holds it before him for a few moments.

"I'm working on a problem right now," he says at last. "I'm an alcoholic. I used to drink so I could block out the pain I felt in my life. Later I just became numb to everything—I couldn't feel anything, pain or joy. At that point I drank and did drugs so I could loosen up and feel something. Now I'm working on staying sober. It's strange, but listening to you guys and even just holding this stick shows me that there are other ways besides the booze that I can connect with what I'm feeling. That's good to know. That's something I need to learn. Maybe this weekend will help me learn that—and remember it."

A voice says "ho," and the stick changes hands....

"I was going to introduce myself as Junior," says the next man. "That's what my parents call me, and that's what I've been known as all my life. But lately that name has made me uncomfortable. Being called 'Junior' makes me feel, I don't know, small or second-class. I don't think I'll ever feel like a grownup guy as long as I have that name. Tonight seems like the right time to start using my real name. So I'd like you to know me as David, since from now on that's who I want to be."

The stick moves on....

"I'm Tom," says the next to speak. "When I heard about this weekend—a bunch of guys sitting around talking—I didn't want to come. But then I remembered that during my tour of duty in Vietnam the best times were when it was just me and my tent buddy. We talked for hours about everything. I never thought you could get so close to someone. Then one day I watched him get his ass shot off. He bled to death in my arms. Something inside me died that day, too. I came here because I thought I might get some of that back."

Someone says "ho." So do others. The stick is passed....

Phil says, "Waiting for that stick to get to me, I thought, this Talking Stick thing is stupid—I'm not going to say anything. I'll just pass the stick to the next guy. But now that I'm holding the stick, I see that it really works. I'm pretty impressed with the way some of you guys have opened up and let us know what's on your minds. I thought men weren't supposed to be able to do that. You've given me the courage to speak up." And he tells of the secret shame he has carried but never before voiced: that for years, until he was 14, he had been sexually abused by the family babysitter. The inner scars from that experience, he says, have kept him from forming any lasting intimate relationships with women. He is lonely, he says. "But just now, being in this room with people who are listening to me, and not judging me—well, somehow I don't feel so lonely anymore."

The journey of the Talking Stick continues. Brad...Dana ...Chuck...Ed....Some speak of pain, some of joy; some tell of longings, others of fears, still others of the burdens they bear. Whatever their words, theirs is the new voice of men.

Some hours later, the time for words has passed. The stick passes around the circle once more, this time in silence. The leader places the stick back into its leather sheath. Saying goodnight, the men move off into the darkness.

The healing has begun.

Chapter 1

THE DISPOSABLE MALE

Allan glanced at the clock. Just one more hour and his shift at the petroleum refinery would end. He was tired and wanted to get home.

Suddenly hell happened. There was an explosion. A huge tank burst into a fireball. The force of the blast knocked Allan off his feet. He was lucky—nearly two dozen workers died.

The next day, though still pretty shaken up, he returned to the site of the accident. Oily smoke choked the air. Buildings had been leveled. Some women employees asked him to get their belongings inside one of the damaged buildings. In his gut Allan didn't want to go anywhere near those structures, but he didn't want to look like a coward either. So he braced himself and went to the rescue. Later he hid behind some bushes and threw up.

The image of the explosion burned itself into Allan's brain. In the days to come he relived the experience—every thought, every feeling—a hundred times. Months later he was still having nightmares. He was tense and angry around his wife and kids. He couldn't concentrate on his job and became anxious when it was time to go to work each day. He became severely depressed. Fortunately, someone in the personnel office realized what was happening and told him where to go for help.

Allan was admitted to our treatment program at Baywood Hospital, a program that focuses on men and their needs. Early in the program, during a group therapy session, Allan spoke about the explosion. "I was sure I was going to die," he said, his voice chalky and distant. "But somehow I didn't. I saw some of the bodies of the guys that didn't make it. I knew each and every one of them. I had worked with most of them for twelve years."

Someone in the group asked Allan, "How do you feel about what happened?"

Allan thought for a long moment. "Numb," was all he could say.

After a few weeks in treatment, Allan attended an Emerging Male weekend. At one point he brought up the topic of the plant explosion. "I've learned something in this group," he said. "Before, I told everybody I felt numb about the accident. I know now that numbness is really fear and shock. I came an inch away from death and I'm scared that it will happen again. And I'm sad that so many people got hurt and I feel guilty that I survived. I'm also mad as hell that the company let those guys get killed. They just threw them away like bent nails.

"It's weird, but the thing I keep focusing on is that I went *back* to that hellhole the next day like a damned errand boy. It wasn't enough I nearly died working next to a hundred-foot-diameter time bomb. I volunteered to clean up after it, too. And I went back into the building because some women asked me to and I didn't want to look like a pansy. Men are *supposed* to be brave and strong. Men aren't supposed to be afraid. So I went back in. I acted like the big macho protector, when the truth was that *I* was the one who needed a little protecting just then. Maybe if I'd been a real man, I would have said no to everybody. I wouldn't have taken such a dangerous job in the first place. And maybe I wouldn't be needing help today."

Allan learned a bitter lesson: In today's society, he is, as Warren Farrell, author of *Why Men Are the Way They Are* put it, *a disposable male*. He is truly a man of the 1990s: confused about his roles, concerned about his feelings of powerlessness, wondering what it really means to be a man.

Allan is not alone. Millions of men experience the same range of feelings, but don't know where to turn for help.

That's why we started the Men's Forum, a program of treatment exclusively for men. At this point, let us explain who "we" are.

FROM OUR POINT OF VIEW

This book reflects the collective experience of the psychiatrists and psychotherapists on the staff of both the Wetcher Clinic and Baywood Hospital in Houston, Texas.

As founder of the Wetcher Clinic and chief author of this book, I have been practicing psychiatry in the area since the early 1970s. In the past few years a number of therapists have joined my staff who bring with them a special expertise in dealing with men's issues. Art Barker, one of my coauthors, retired from the military after twenty-five years of service in order to return to school and earn a degree. He became a therapist for addiction and family problems, specializing in the treatment of men. My other coauthor, Rex McCaughtry, had been a management consultant for many years. Finding life in the business world unfulfilling, Rex, like Art, went back to school in his mid-40s, earned a master's degree in social work, and changed careers. Working as a team with others on the clinic staff, we realized that we had something special to offer the men in our part of the country. We pooled our talents and created the Men's Forum.

This book is a pooling of talents as well. The term "we" indicates our collective point of view, even though we weren't always together when the events described took place. Also, as members of the community of men, we are in part the subjects of our own book. It seems right to use "we" because our own lives are affected by the same concerns that men wrestle with today.

TO SAVE THE MALES

Traditionally, most of the people who come in for therapy and counseling are women. It didn't make sense to us, however, that women should necessarily have more problems than men. Something must have been keeping men away. The few men who did come in were from many different walks of life: business executives, factory workers, military men, maritime crews. Yet they all had something in common, something that didn't appear in the psychiatric textbooks. Generally, their problems arose from their perceptions—and misperceptions—of themselves as men.

We realized that men were resisting treatment because they felt ashamed. Men in our society are taught that it isn't macho to feel pain, let alone tell someone that they are hurting. Yet standard therapy was often directed at the very area where men are considered weakest: recognizing and expressing their feelings. Men in traditional treatment, especially in group treatment with women, were made to feel like failures, first for being out of touch with their emotions, and second for having trouble talking about those emotions.

At the same time, men were suffering in great numbers from such problems as depression, substance abuse, alcoholism, and so on. Society had been slowly catching on to the fact that such people need help, not criticism. Many companies created Employee Assistance Programs to steer their workers toward the treatment they needed.

For years women have been successfully treated in groups for women only. The time seemed right for an experiment—to find the best way to Save the Males.

That's why we launched the Men's Forum, the first successful inpatient program in the country devoted to helping men learn about themselves, their thoughts and feelings, their values and expectations. Success has enabled us to expand enormously. We now have many men's outpatient groups that meet at the Wetcher Clinic, as well as an all-men's unit at Baywood Hospital. We also offer programs for the community at large, such as the Emerging Male weekends described in the prologue, about which we'll say more in the final chapter of this book.

The results of our experiment have been astounding. Men now have a safe place where they can come and explore their lives in the company of other men. We teach men to look at their problems in the broadest possible context. We show how pressures from work, from relationships, and from family responsibilities combine to create conflict and confusion. We bring men together so they can help each other deal with problems in an environment that only men can provide.

We take what we call a *gender-specific* approach to psychiatric problems. That means we teach men that their reactions to events—and thus the way they attempt to solve problems—are directly affected by the way society has taught them to be men. Once they see how restrictive these gender roles and expectations can be, they can begin the work of freeing themselves from these roles and trying on newer, healthier ones.

Some problems that are exclusive to men, and thus respond to a gender-specific approach, are:

- The demands of being a father
- Responsibilities of being a husband
- Unsatisfactory or unfulfilling relationship between a son and a father
- Defining self-esteem exclusively in terms of competition with other men
- Pressure to create a "financial womb" to make one's family feel secure
- Establishing relationships with women—being assertive and powerful yet intimate
- Dealing with rejection from women

- Building close friendships with men

Other types of problems are not exclusive to men, but men react to them in a different way than women. Among these are:

- Using rage and aggressiveness as a means of coping with loss of control and feelings of powerlessness
- Dealing and competing with women in the workplace
- Denying pain rather than risk appearing dependent or weak
- Reverting to silence and withdrawing rather than expressing sadness or other emotions
- Diverting feelings by becoming obsessed with work or hobbies
- Handling failure in a world devoted to success

We feel qualified to teach men this new way of seeing because we have "walked a mile in their moccasins." We are married and have raised children of our own. We have taken on traditional male roles—husbands, providers, soldiers, businessmen—and have learned how to be flexible when an old role is no longer satisfying. We have grown, too, through our own work in the program. When we conduct an Emerging Male weekend, for example, we are not just leaders; we are active participants. We also make it a point to be involved in the currently widening network of other people devoted to helping men. We attend conventions, make presentations, take part in men's weekends led by nationally known figures, and work closely with other therapists interested in men's issues.

We are writing this book to share what we have learned thus far. In doing so we hope to achieve several goals: to help men understand the issues that confront them; to explain how these problems arise; and to point out ways of resolving them.

THE DISPOSABLE MALE

Will we be able to save the males?
While the answer is by no means clear, we do know we urgently have to try. Men are dying—spiritually, emotionally, and physically. In the year 1900, men tended to die two years earlier than women. Today, despite advances in the quality and availability of health care, *men are dying seven or eight years sooner than women*. One study predicts that

by the year 2000, the gap in life expectancy between the sexes will be as great as ten years. Such traditional male characteristics as exposure to stress, competition, aggressiveness, and restrained emotional expression contribute to this premature death.

Somehow society has decided that men are the disposable sex. Perhaps this attitude arises from the biological fact that, strictly speaking, there are a lot more men around than are really needed in order for the human species to propagate and survive.

Men experience their disposability in dozens of ways. They are society's sacrificial animals, taking on dangerous and stressful jobs to support their families. As Allan put it, they become "a piece of meat for an income." Obviously there are rewards that are intended to compensate for these risks—money, prestige, and power to make choices and act on them. But, as Allan remarked, "There isn't enough money in the world to get me back up on one of those oil tanks." Many men find themselves in Allan's position—putting their lives on the line at enormous physical and emotional cost.

These are the males that need to be saved. To do so, we must explore and redefine the roles that men and women play in today's society.

BALL OF CONFUSION

Men today are in a state of crisis. They struggle with the difficulties of earning a living. They are taught they must fight like hell in the jungle of the workplace, then come home, switch gears, and try to be loving and caring to their wife and kids. Men today often sacrifice their own most cherished dreams to provide security and stability for others in their care. At the same time many of them try in good faith to understand the changes women are experiencing and to adjust to those changes as best they can.

Even so, many men feel they are under attack simply because of the sex chromosomes they inherited at the moment they were conceived in the womb. For many people, masculinity has become the symbol of everything wrong with contemporary Western society: men have made our world too rationalistic, militaristic, materialistic, and competitive. During the 1970s, masculinity became synonymous with evil. After all, men were the "cause" of war, pollution, and inequality, weren't they? If we just didn't have men, this line of thinking goes, then everything would be fine.

Certainly men have assumed the lion's share of responsibility for creating our civilization, and are thus entitled to their share of the blame for its mistakes. And without doubt men have much room for improvement in their attitudes and values.

Nonetheless, we must be fair to men by recognizing that currently they are being pulled in all directions. Men are told:

"Be kind and understanding—but don't be a wimp."

"Spend more time with the kids—but don't lose out on that promotion."

"Be emotional—but don't lose control."

We tend to forget that the male role has evolved over thousands of years. Many male characteristics were reinforced, generation after generation. For all those millennia, male traits contributed a great deal, making it possible for humans to survive as a species. It may be true that certain of these traits are no longer necessary, at least not to the same degree they once were. For example, just as we no longer need to hunt and gather in order to survive, we could certainly do with a less aggressive stance toward our fellow human beings. But to expect total, dramatic, revolutionary change overnight is simply not possible, nor would it even be desirable.

No wonder men are confused. Where can they turn for answers about what it means to be a man?

THE SEARCH FOR ANSWERS

Until the modern industrial age, the father was the main model for maleness. Today, however, men are commonly absent from the family scene. Many men work long hours or double shifts to provide for their families, and are thus absent during most of their children's waking hours. There are also many households with only one parent, usually the mother. As a result of this "absent father" phenomenon, there are shockingly high numbers of children who are being raised without the influence of a strong male figure in their lives.

Sigmund Freud observed that it is necessary in a boy's healthy development for him to experience a period of struggle against his father. In the process, according to Freud, the boy comes to renounce the mother and identify with the father. As he does, he adopts the father's male characteristics, thus taking on the values and standards set for men by society. Many of the psychological conflicts men wrestle with today, and that we will no doubt see more of in the coming years, stem from a lack of strong fathering. In countless therapy sessions, encounter groups, and private conversations, we often hear the tragic refrain: "My father wasn't there for me."

The image-makers of Hollywood and Madison Avenue eagerly supply their version of the Real Man. In one era we are told that John Wayne is the model of masculinity: tight-lipped, gung-ho, no-nonsense. In another era we learn to be like Alan Alda: sweet, witty, cuddly, "sensitive." But wait—now we have the new, improved Male Model for the 1990s: Kevin Costner, sensitive yet strong, rugged yet tender, quiet but articulate, reserved yet expressive, normal but extraordinary.

Quite a lot to live up to!

For many years the field of psychiatry, devoted as it is to helping people cope with emotional problems, missed an opportunity to make a difference in men's lives. Psychotherapy works by uncovering the hidden feelings and motivations that direct our thoughts and behaviors.

Unfortunately for men, the language of feelings proved to be more useful in helping women because women were socialized to talk and think in *terms* of feelings. Psychiatrists tended to be more aware of women's needs and thus developed techniques to help them. As a result, at any given time, perhaps as many as *eight out of ten patients in psychiatric care are women*. This isn't to say that women have a higher incidence of mental illness. On the contrary, the numbers are roughly equal (although the diagnoses given men and women can vary widely). It's closer to the truth to say that some of the psychiatric methods currently available are simply of little value to men. And even if these methods were ideal, men are taught that it isn't manly to ask for help. They're told if they have a problem, just deal with it themselves. If they fail—well, men are disposable anyway.

Lately men have been turning to ancient myths and poetry to learn what it means to be a man. The psychologist Carl Jung and the mythologist Joseph Campbell demonstrated that ancient symbols and legends hold powerful clues to the male and female forces at work in the universe. Drawing on their work, as well as on ancient folk tales, the poet Robert Bly uses verse to explore the meaning of maleness. In our own work as psychotherapists we have combined some of these mythical and poetic elements with a medical approach to men's problems. The results, which we will share in this book, have been extremely encouraging.

REMOVING MEN FROM RISK

We will explain how society creates its stereotypes of men and how men learn what is expected of them. We will also look at the contribution biology makes to the male mode of being. We will then examine the unfortunate outcomes of gender role strain, especially the psychological disorders that can result. Our purpose in identifying these problems is to point the way toward solutions. In so doing we will show how addressing problems from the perspective of gender can free men from their unhealthy and constricting roles. We will see how honoring male virtues and achieving a balance in male and female attitudes can produce healthy emotionality, closer personal relationships, the blessings of friendship, achievement through cooperation as well as competition, mental health, and a longer, more satisfying life.

As we've noted, part of our treatment program includes the Emerging Male weekends. The name is apt. We want to encourage men to break through the shells that society has constructed for them and emerge into the light. Doing so means taking risks—but that is something men do pretty well. Our methods are based on established and accepted psychiatric practice, involving inpatient and outpatient programs offering various kinds of therapy. But we go a step farther, tapping into men's inner strength and wisdom by creating a community exclusively of and for men who validate each other by creating a sense of brotherhood and belonging. Our goal is not soft men but *whole* men.

We anticipate that some people will reject the ideas in this book out of hand. For example, it is difficult for some to accept that there are significant differences between men and women. Their concern is valid; too many times "differences" can be misinterpreted to mean that certain traits grant *superiority* to one sex over the other, which in turn can lead to greater social bias and restrictiveness. We will make the case, however, that such differences do exist, that they are important, and that honoring the special virtues of maleness does not detract from the special virtues of femaleness.

Others may object by stating that men have held a disproportionate share of power in society for long enough, and that the last thing we need is more emphasis on men and their needs. Concentrating on men's problems, this argument goes, shifts focus and resources away from women's issues. We would suggest instead that helping men resolve their conflicts will go a long way toward addressing many of the complaints women have justifiably lodged against men. Teaching men, for example, that anger and violence or withdrawal are not their only options for emotional expression will contribute much to women's sense of safety and will lead to happier relationships between the sexes.

Another concern is that a men's therapy program will be perceived as nothing but a forum for "women bashing." The truth is, the field of psychotherapy has for some time now been drifting toward a relentless campaign of *male* bashing. We agree that men have been responsible for some grievous offenses against women, ranging from job discrimination to abuse to rape. In reality, men and women, under the sway of socialization, hurt each other in different ways. Our approach is to explore the ways that society creates a harmful male stereotype. By emphasizing the role of the cultural environment, we address an enemy that is much greater and much more powerful than men or women alone. As Warren Farrell states in his book *Why Men Are the Way They Are*, "This dilemma is no one's fault; we are all innocently born into a system in motion."

We believe that psychiatry has been "gender-blind" too long. Assessing and treating men and women as if they were the same does not produce the best results. Bringing about change means exploring the roles men fall into and teaching them new, less destructive alternatives. Often those best qualified to teach a man are other men. They already talk male talk.

Let there be no misunderstanding: Women are a vital asset in a well-rounded treatment program for men because of their intelligence, insight, and compassion. They are fully qualified to address issues of male sexuality. As one woman psychotherapist put it, she can approach the subject as a biographer would, which is a different but no less valuable method than autobiography. To achieve full understanding, men need therapy, mentoring, and teaching from women as well as other men.

But there are times when a man needs to be with other men in a noncompetitive setting in order to feel safe. He can express himself without fear of being seen as a chauvinist or a whiner or a wimp. The mere presence of a woman changes the group's dynamics, in part by increasing the type and intensity of competition. In all-men groups, relationships can grow without the static that a sexually charged environment can produce. The sympathetic presence of other men who listen without judging and who share the burden can be an incredibly empowering experience.

Creating a new psychology of men allows us to explore, develop, and integrate the many basic elements that exist within each man. Jung called these elements the *archetypes,* which have been described as "a treasure of seeds within the self." Various names have been given to these archetypes; the psychoanalyst Robert Moore, for example, mentions the King, the Warrior, the Magician, the Lover, and the Wild Man. In a way, a gender-based method of solving men's problems serves some of the needs that rites of initiation address in primitive cultures. Such a method eases the transition into manhood by nurturing those seeds within and helping men grow to maturity.

Through this approach men benefit by becoming fully realized men. Women will benefit by finding partners worthy of their love. But the ones who stand to benefit most, perhaps, are the children. They will have new male role models to look up to and with whom to identify. They will have the chance to grow up free of outdated and dangerous gender stereotypes. They are the seeds that the new man, in his turn, will nurture.

Chapter 2

The Male Stereotype

"Gender" means everything that relates to maleness or femaleness. The sex organs are just one component of gender. There are many other elements as well: biological, psychological, and social. As we humans grow and learn, we absorb from our social environment its view of what being a man or a woman is all about. In time we develop our own attitudes and act accordingly. We develop, in other words, a gender identity.

The distinction between "sex" and "gender" is crucial. There are (discounting rare chromosomal abnormalities) only two sexes: male and female. Yet each person, regardless of sex, contains a unique mix of many different male and female attributes. There are as many gender identities as there are people on the planet.

The point is that one's sex is determined by biology, while one's gender is determined by biology interacting with culture. Culture is the way society communicates its views, for better or worse, through such institutions as family, religion, government, and education. We might think of gender as the way a society and its individual members *interpret* the meaning of sex. The way people act out these interpretations is their psychology.

Society places expectations on people depending on their sex. We refer to these expectations as *gender roles*. Like an actor's script, a role specifies a set of behaviors and responsibilities that exist in relationships with other individuals. By taking on roles, people create larger social entities: marriages (where the roles are husband and wife), families (fathers, mothers, children), peer groups (friends, opponents), and work groups (employers, employees).

These larger social entities take on a kind of life of their own, making demands on the people involved. Ideally, the interests and needs of the individual and their social entities are compatible—but not always. What's more, those needs may change over time. A gender role may suddenly be rewritten, leaving the individual who is trying to fulfill that role confused and frustrated. Sometimes people get stuck in the wrong role when they encounter a situation. For example, a businessman may treat his children more as employees than as family members. Gender-specific therapy is aimed at discovering what those roles are and how to best fulfill them without causing pain and confusion.

To understand gender roles, we have to understand how society creates those roles. Throughout this book we will see that society's definition of the male gender role—what it means to be a man—is not always healthy. In fact, it can be downright dangerous. If a culture's view of gender is too rigid, too demanding, too much at odds with reality, the results can be disastrous. Also, men may need to learn how to choose the best role for themselves in each situation. Therapy is nothing more than teaching men a wider range of choices in their reactions.

The basic message of the women's movement has been that outdated or false views about the meaning of gender contribute to oppression and unhappiness. Our goal in this book is to make the same case for men.

The social changes brought about by women are improving the situation for everybody. But we haven't yet reached full equality, and we won't until we also address the gender issues that *men* must wrestle with—issues that for too long have been ignored or considered unworthy of attention.

In our experience as therapists, we find that men, too, can be victimized by society's narrow view of their roles. Many of the problems men experience—troubled relationships, depression, substance abuse, rage, illness, early death—are often the direct result of gender-related stress. We want to teach men that they must resist being typecast and must learn to try out new roles that offer greater happiness and potential for fulfillment. We want to help them to understand and choose the best role for each situation. True freedom is the ability to make choices. The results will benefit not just men, but the women who love them, the families of which they are part, and the society that thrives on their energy and their virtues.

MALE PORTRAITS

A stereotype is a group portrait that tries to squeeze everyone into the picture. Stereotypes convey only the broadest outline and omit individual details. They are dangerous because people, confusing the stereotype for the reality, base their thoughts and actions on an incomplete and simplistic picture.

They are also dangerous because they contain small amounts of truth. We ignore the reality behind stereotypes at our peril.

What is the male stereotype?

A man is strong. He must be given the heaviest load to carry. No matter that his strength gives out in time. If he refuses to shoulder what society declares is his share of the burden—well, he is not a man.

A man is aggressive. He must take charge and dominate others and his environment. If he does not stand up and fight, if he prefers to negotiate to reach a consensus—he is not a man.

A man is competitive. He must pitch himself against the forces of the world. True, only one of the combatants can emerge victorious. The one who is defeated—he is not a man.

A man is active. He bases his identity on the things he does. If he is passive or refuses to take charge—he is not a man.

A man is powerful. He devotes his energies to dominating others and imposing his view of reality on them. A man who feels weak at times, who wishes to retreat or to lean on someone else for a while—he is not a man.

A man is self-reliant. He refuses to recognize his connection to other people. If he calls on another for help, if he looks to others for answers—he is not a man.

A man is adventurous. He takes chances; he sticks his neck out. In the mating ritual, it is he who must take the risks, make the first phone call, guide the relationship toward sexual intimacy. If he opts at times not to take risks, not to explore unknown territory—he is not a man.

A man is successful. He sets goals only to reach them. If he should fail—he is not a man.

A man is emotionally restrained. He must not show his emotions because that would reveal his vulnerable spots. If he expresses his feelings, indeed if he even knows what his feelings are—he is not a man.

Society transforms these stereotyped gender traits into the roles it expects men to play: risk-takers, breadwinners, leaders, soldiers, explorers, loners. We'll explore this transformation in the next chapter.

There's no denying that certain "male" qualities—strength, self-reliance, control—are sometimes very useful, even essential, to society. Doers get things done. Breadwinners bring home food that lets the family survive. Explorers expand our horizons.

The problem is that such roles, although valuable, can also be extremely stressful, if not downright hazardous. Men are taught that they have to be this way in all of their dealings with others. Yet no one can fulfill the requirements of such demanding roles perfectly and at all times. Even were that possible, the damage to the body and to the soul would be incalculable.

When a man senses he has failed in his role, he suffers doubly—once by failing and twice by not comprehending why he failed. Not seeing that the role may have been inappropriate for him in the first place, he may lash out angrily. He may turn to alcohol or other drugs for relief. He may withdraw even further into his emotional shell. Unfortunately, society, having created the problem, often compounds it by failing to help that man overcome his suffering.

Like the actor who doesn't fit the part, a man who fails to learn his social script properly is seen as a failure and is dismissed from the cast. He is a loser, a weakling. He will not have the respect of other men or the love of women. Worse, he will not respect or love himself.

GENDER ROLE STRAIN

Researchers have identified and described an entire gender role strain syndrome. Not so strangely, many of the "symptoms" they describe also appear on the list of classic male traits that have fostered the male stereotype:

- Restrictive emotionality
- Emphasis on control, power, and competition
- Homophobia
- Restrictive sexual and affectionate behavior
- Obsession with achievement and success
- Health care problems

Let's look at these symptoms in more detail.

When we say men restrict their emotions, we mean that they not only lack the ability to express feelings, they may also lack any understanding of what their feelings are. As Allan's story in Chapter 1 demonstrated, he crammed all his feelings about the plant explosion into one emotional box and filed it away under the label "numbness." Through therapy he was able to identify and express his true feelings: fear, sadness, guilt, anger.

As the second symptom indicates, many men have been socialized to believe that the only way they can prove their masculinity is by dominating and triumphing over others. Men often struggle to put themselves "one-up" in their dealings with other people. They play what some have called a "zero-sum" game: for every winner there must be a loser.

Homophobia doesn't necessarily mean that "real men hate homosexuals," although that line still appears often, and in boldface, in society's script for the male gender role. Instead homophobia means that many men refuse or are unable to become emotionally intimate with other men for fear of being perceived as feminine or gay. The truth is, no one understands a man better than another man. Men who can't connect emotionally are two-time losers: They lack a healthy way of letting their feelings show, and they miss out on a chance to learn from the wisdom of other men.

For many men, sex is a matter of performance and dominance over women. They are concerned about how they are doing, not with what their partner is feeling. Many men have to be "on top," physically and emotionally, or they can't enjoy sex. If women are aggressive or take control of the sexual agenda, some men may feel threatened or ashamed. Men miss out on fully half of their sexual pleasure if they fail to develop their sensuality and their ability to achieve intimacy.

There's nothing inherently wrong with desiring success, the fifth symptom on the list. The trouble comes when that desire leads to a persistent and disturbing preoccupation with work, accomplishment, and position in the world. Workaholics, as the label suggests, are addicted to their jobs, placing them ahead of every other important relationship in their lives. Many successful men reach the top of the ladder only to find themselves feeling lonely and unfulfilled.

The last symptom is in many ways the most disturbing. Sometimes the only visible sign that a man is suffering from gender role strain is an increase in health problems.

The increasing gap between male and female life expectancies, which was cited earlier, is strong evidence that being a male can be hazardous to one's health. Men are experts at ignoring their pain because their role, as scripted by society, doesn't allow them to get sick. Being sick is not "macho." Even as young boys they learn that they have to "play with the pain" and that "only sissies get hurt."

As adults, many men neglect their nutrition and fail to exercise. They subject themselves to enormous amounts of stress, but know next to nothing about managing it. A body under constant stress wears out, the immune system weakens, and the organs quit working.

Nevertheless, men visit doctors far *less* frequently than women. After all, they have been conditioned not to ask for help or give up control of their situation to another person. Consequently, when they finally do seek medical help, their illness or injury is much worse than it would have been had they taken care of it sooner. After age 50 men are hospitalized at a higher rate than women; they are sicker, must stay longer, and require more hours of nursing. The ratio of male and female deaths from lung cancer is six to one; five times as many men die of other pulmonary diseases; four times as many men die from homicides; two and a half times as many men die from suicides or motor vehicle accidents. It's interesting to note that as more and more women enter the workplace and assume the responsibilities and pressures that only men used to encounter, the incidence of stress-related illness, including heart disease, has increased significantly among women.

Our emphasis in this book will be on the psychiatric fallout from gender role strain. We will see how certain men's problems, such as substance abuse, post-traumatic stress, unhealthy interpersonal relationships, depression, and suicide can be understood—and addressed—as the consequences of being locked into an unhealthy, but socially reinforced, pattern of behavior.

MALE AND FEMALE

Despite the confusion of voices, one clear theme is emerging in the discussion about gender roles and stereotypes. Society has rediscovered the ancient idea that each person contains a mix of male and female attributes. The healthiest people are those who recognize that both of these forces are operating within them in a never-ending cycle. Sometimes the male predominates, sometimes the female.

Some men, ashamed of the damage that male traits have sometimes caused, go to extreme lengths to deny their manliness and cultivate their female side. Recently, for example, a speaker at a professional gathering announced that he was a "recovering male," as if maleness were an addiction, of which men must be cured!

We believe that, on the contrary, there is much to be

honored about maleness. If we are to save the males, we must work to identify and preserve that which is good about their nature. We must also nurture that which is good about the female in men. Finally, we must move beyond this simple duality and recognize that true humanity consists not just of two states, but, as Robert Bly puts it, "all sorts of degrees, intermediate states, unions, combinations, special cases, genius exceptions, and so on." In the process we will free ourselves from the constrictions of gender roles and develop a new repertoire of flexible responses to the challenges of living.

MEN: WORTH SAVING

Many things about men have value. Even the traits for which men are often criticized have some positive aspects.

Aggression, for example, is perhaps the most criticized male trait. Without aggression we would have no wars, no rape, no violence or brutality. At the same time we would have nothing to compel us to defend ourselves or our families when attacked. We would lack the drive to provide for our basic needs, such as food and shelter. Without a healthy level of aggression, even the mating dance would grind to a halt, and our species would fade from the scene in a blur of passivity and languor. Some degree of aggression is essential to our survival.

Men are also accused of being "too logical." But approaching problems through rational thinking, rather than emotional responses, can lead to solutions that are more fair, more complete, more accurate, and longer-lasting. Of course, some have argued that rational thinking also produced the atomic bomb. But male traits should not be discarded merely because at first blush there appear to be some negative components. Better to bring those negative components into consciousness and get control of them, rather than be controlled by them.

When men keep their emotions to themselves, they can drive their wives or their friends crazy. Nonetheless, in the midst of a crisis, it is that very ability to keep calm that we depend on. At the right time, restricted emotionality can be a plus.

Men are thought to be rigid in their beliefs, sometimes fighting to the death for the sake of principle. Yet conviction moves mountains and directs the course of nations. It also drives a man to bond with a woman and devote himself exclusively to her. Fidelity is a form of rigidity many people prize.

Frequently men are blasted for being so devoted to their work. What is often overlooked, however, is that for many men, work is their direct way of expressing commitment to their families. A man may not say "I love you" often enough, he may not bring home flowers or act romantic at just the right times. For many men, however, putting in long hours and depositing the paycheck every Friday says it all.

Men are ridiculed for their fascination with sports and games. Sure, their constant interest in competition can become tiresome. But, as author Warren Farrell points out, sports teach men an appreciation for rules and the wisdom of fair play. Because everybody plays by the same rules, everybody—theoretically, anyway—has an equal chance of success. Playing on teams helps men realize they can compete fiercely with one another for a period of time, and then knock off to go socialize together. Some women in business are perplexed by this phenomenon, because they find they are unable to set aside their feelings of competitiveness at quitting time.

Anger is the emotion men are most likely to express. Uncontrolled anger is emotionally and physically damaging. However, anger is a genuine human response that must be acknowledged as necessary, even healthy. Anger signals that something cherished is under threat. Recognizing that threat empowers a man to deflect it. When men channel their anger properly, it serves as a force for constructive change.

Sometimes men are criticized for being too quick to act. Certainly there are times when more deliberation would be the wiser course, but inaction leads to inertia, stagnation, and death.

The male tendency to take risks has led to such forms of insanity as Russian roulette and games of "chicken" played on a global scale. But risk-taking also creates progress in everything, from new industries to new modes of artistic expression.

Men also bring a special quality to the nurturing of children. Their style is different from that of the nurturing of a mother, but no less valid, as Dr. Kyle Pruett explains in his book *The Nurturing Father*. Men encourage children to experience the world and explore its outer limits, guiding them to the edge of the cliff but not letting them fall off. Men nurture grown children by helping them leave home when the time is right but making it clear they are standing by in case of trouble.

One last point: Men have feelings, too. So pervasive is the myth of the unemotional man that society sometimes is blind to the subtle ways a man does express himself. Often a man states what he is feeling, only to be condemned for having that emotion. (There is a cartoon, featuring a married couple called "The Lockhorns," in which the husband says, "I *am* in touch with my feelings. You just don't happen to like the feelings I'm in touch with.") Or he states his feelings in terms of thoughts, which are then discounted. In our practice we make a special effort to listen to the emotional voice and language of men. When men believe they will be truly heard, they are more willing to speak.

As in most stereotypes, there is some truth to the stereotype of men. What's important, however, is not to assume that a stereotype represents the *whole* truth. Doing so discounts the value of the individual man and places him at risk.

Chapter 3

The Power of Socialization

Be a man!

"Play with the pain!" the coach shouts at an injured player. "Get off your butt and get back on the field!"

"Big boys don't cry," Mama says, wiping her 8-year-old's cheek.

Real Men Don't Eat Quiche reads the title of a book published a few years ago.

"What are you, a man or a mouse?" the father yells at the kid perched at the edge of the high diving board, mustering his strength to plunge into the cold water far below. "Come on, sissy."

These messages, the dozens more like them, are society's way of telling men what is expected of them. Like blazes on a trail, these cues guide men through their roles in life, showing them how to think, act, and feel.

Socialization—the process of teaching us what and how to be—is the most powerful and pervasive force in the making of a man. Biology counts for a lot, too, as we'll see in the next chapter. But in most cases socialization can be strong enough to override even the most basic biological impulses.

To understand how this can be, consider the fact that some people are born with the genetic tendency to develop high cholesterol. If they were also socialized to eat fried fast food, and sit around the office during the day and in front of the television at night, their cholesterol problem would get worse and their risk of heart disease would increase. Those socialized to care for their health through diet, exercise, and the use of medication, however, can overcome that biological trait.

Since society is such a powerful force, it is important that we design workable roles for its members. Those roles must not clash with nature to the degree that they become impossible to achieve. To give a ridiculous example, a society will not last very long if it declares that all of its men must either have operatic singing voices or die. Such a culture would not be able to sustain itself for very long.

Yet socialization does place enormous burdens on men's shoulders by telling them they must always be strong, aggressive, active, powerful, and in control. Many men struggle to fulfill these demands, in actuality or in their own self-perception. Those who fail fall by the wayside and are abandoned.

Every human civilization that has sprung up has been based to some degree on sex-role differences. Some people argue that sex roles are nothing more than reflections of the psychological characteristics with which men and women are born. The evidence is strong, however, that social roles actually *create* some of those characteristics. In other words, the seemingly sex-related aspects of our personalities are largely the product of our interaction with society.

In most societies, men are given the role of the "family's representatives in the outside world," while women tend to the family's physical and emotional needs. As the family's agent, the man is expected to be independent and self-reliant; as the caregiver, the woman develops her nurturing skills and her ability to express and respond to emotions. As we've said, however, these roles are not necessarily connected directly to a person's sex. In those rare societies in which the roles are reversed and the man is in charge of the family, men become expressive and nurturant while women become active and aggressive. The point is that a society, if it chooses to, can make nurturance and emotional expressiveness a goal for its men.

WHERE MEN ARE MEN

How does our own culture teach its men what to be? What powerful processes are at work to mold them into the type of human beings society decides are valuable?

There are many forces that combine to make us who we are. Our parents are the first and in many ways the most powerful influence. A boy looks to his father to learn what it means to be a man. For good or ill, a father is the boy's role model, the embodiment of society's vision of manhood. Throughout his life the boy will compare himself against his image of his father. If that father is missing from the household, or if his contact with his son is minimal and filled with conflict, the child must look elsewhere.

Television and movies are another important source of

images about manhood. A child who watches cartoons about Ninja turtles rescuing helpless women will soon graduate to films where machine gun-toting muscle men single-handedly wipe out the enemy and save civilization. At the end of each seven-minute cartoon or ninety-minute movie, the hero, victorious, is rewarded with a grateful kiss by the damsel-in-distress.

Peer pressure reinforces the messages children absorb. A young boy may be happily involved in a dance class, but once his older brother or a friend taunts him by calling him a "sissy," he may never dance another step. On the playground, games are devoted to creating an informal pecking order, a hierarchy of winners and losers. It doesn't take long for the athletically gifted to find their niche at the top, a position they reinforce as team leaders when they choose up sides and pick the weakest players last—or not at all. As Warren Farrell notes, cheerleaders root for their heroes, but if the hero is hurt during the game, he is carried off, disposed of, and replaced by another male body in a uniform, like the interchangeable parts of an automobile.

As boys grow, they usually must find their way through the sexual jungle without much helpful guidance. Fathers may tell them the facts of life, but they aren't as good at preparing boys for the *feelings* of life. Boys learn that they are expected to be the aggressors, initiating relationships with girls and bearing the risks and burdens of potential rejection. Because they have been brought up in a society that emphasizes competition, they tend to see relationships in terms of a contest. That's why there is so much pressure for guys to "score" with their dates. They are eager to report sexual victories so that they can be accepted by their buddies as one of the team. Sex becomes a source, not of mutual respect and pleasure between a male and female, but of "points" on a social scoreboard.

Our society is pretty effective at getting across its narrow image of what men are supposed to be. It isn't as good at teaching men how to develop intimacy, how to be gentle and caring, how to deal with failure and setbacks. Part of the Male Message is to "keep your feelings to yourself." A boy or a man who feels that something is wrong with the way he is being trained has to keep his mouth shut or risk becoming a social outcast. As we have seen in our psychiatric practice, the consequences of bottling up these feelings include substance abuse, outbursts of anger, physical ailments, and a host of other deadly complications.

THE PATH TO MANHOOD

To understand how we got where we are, let's look back along the road that brought us to our current situation. What follows is a brief summary of how male socialization has shifted over the centuries, especially during the last century and a half. Our aim is to show that society's image of manhood changes as its values and its needs change. Such changes, while sometimes slowly and painfully achieved, give us reason to hope that society, once enlightened, can continue to adjust the way it teaches to promote a healthier, less stressful version of maleness.

The first humans assigned to their men the task of providing food. Since agriculture was still a few millennia away, this usually meant hunting. According to anthropologist Lionel Tiger, while women stayed behind to tend to the young, the men set off in search of game. The more successful groups were those who realized that, by cooperating and combining their skills, the hunters could bag bigger animals and thus provide food for many more people. Some linguists believe that the first use of language may have been to discuss the strategy for the hunt: "You go that way, we'll go this way." For thousands of years this technique for survival worked pretty well.

Eventually humans made it easier on themselves by learning to raise crops and breed animals for consumption. Putting food on the table was a lot simpler when you didn't have to go chasing after it with a sharp stick. Put simply, agriculture brought civilization: People stayed in one place, lived together in communities, created surpluses of food, and learned to trade their surplus for some of the other necessities of life. For the system to work, people needed to cooperate in more ways than ever before—for example, by not killing every stranger who wandered across their path. The primitive instincts, inbred for thousands of years, were concealed beneath a thin veneer of civility. Sometimes, when one culture had something another one wanted, the veneer was stripped away and war erupted. To make sure its men would do well in battle, societies continued breeding men to be tough, aggressive, and fearless.

Flash forward now to the 1700s, the Colonial Era. The typical man worked on the family farm or shop, aided by his wife and their children. Because they were always present, fathers took an active role in rearing the children, particularly their sons. The boys thus had firsthand knowledge of their father's work. They also had before them a model representing society's image of what it meant to be a man.

The Industrial Revolution changed all that. Machines now did the work, and men were needed to tend the machines. Men thus left the home, even their communities, to go to work, leaving the women behind to rear the children. Education was left to the mothers or to schoolteachers, who were mostly women. As early as 1820, social critics noticed that men no longer played a vital role in bringing up children because they were seldom at home.

It was during this era that the world experienced what some have called the "crisis of masculinity." No longer was physical strength an essential male asset, since even the simplest machine could do the work of a dozen men. The family no longer produced the food and supplies they needed; they bought them ready-made. By taking on repetitive, mechanical, specialized jobs, men lost many of the broad skills they had developed. Many people no longer owned the houses or land on which they lived. Before industrialization, women generally worked side-by-side with men, sharing responsibility for the home, family, and labor. Only after industrialization did society create the woman's "traditional" role—full-time homemaker and mother.

In the last half of the nineteenth century, the new models of maleness were the rugged individualists, the entrepreneurs who demonstrated their aggressiveness by seizing opportunities wherever they found them. This was the era of the "self-made man," who controlled society's assets and reaped its many rewards. Of course, there was only so much room at the top. Men who lacked ambition, or who failed in their enterprises, suffered humiliation and defeat.

At the turn of the century men were uncertain about what manliness meant. Many men labored in anonymous niches within huge companies, isolated from any direct contact with the product the company produced, thus finding it harder to acquire the psychological satisfaction needed to define themselves as breadwinners. Men now had virtually no role in bringing up their children; the typical father of the time was seen as little more than a source of paternal advice and, of course, spending money. Before, a man's success had been measured by his strength of character. Now, however, success was measured in terms of wealth. Further challenge to the male image came from the swelling women's reform movement, which demanded, among other things, the right to vote.

World War I—then known as the Great War—was in many ways the death of innocence. Boys enlisted out of a sense of adventure, thinking they were to face the ultimate test of their manliness. America at this time was largely a rural, provincial nation. Most of the doughboys had never been more than a few miles from home. Once they saw the world, their values and perspectives changed. They returned home, having witnessed scenes of mass carnage, stripped of their naïveté and illusions. One casualty of the war was Victorian morality. After the war ended there was a huge jump in the incidence of male neuroses and "nervous breakdowns," a trend attributed to men's inability to adjust to enormous social and sexual changes.

The male role suffered another huge blow during the Great Depression. Men had always found a large part of their identity in their work. By 1932, however, more than twelve million people—mostly men—were out of jobs. No work, no self-esteem. The word "depression" refers to the financial situation, but it might just as easily be applied to the emotional situation. Some of President Roosevelt's New Deal programs helped by offering men the chance to work, even without pay. For many, just having a job to do saved their self-esteem.

With World War II, men again faced the cannons but returned as heroes. In the era of postwar prosperity, writer Barbara Ehrenreich states, "there was firm expectation... that required men to grow up, marry and support their wives. To do anything else was less than grown-up, and the man who willfully deviated was judged to be somehow 'less than a man.'" In fact, so pervasive was this particular gender role image that a poll taken in 1957 found that 53 percent of the American public believed unmarried people were "sick, immoral, or neurotic." Men who couldn't make it as breadwinners supporting families were deemed to have failed as men.

More than ever, men measured themselves by what they did and by what they had. This was the era of "keeping up with the Joneses." Men invested their active energies in their jobs and became increasingly passive at home.

As a way of rebelling against the expectations society placed on them, men had two basic avenues. The first was to buy into the newly developed "playboy" image of free sex, fast cars, and the pursuit of pleasure. "A playboy," Ehrenreich observes, "didn't have to be a husband to be a man." The other avenue was the "beat" movement, whose members rejected not just cozy domesticity but the nine-to-five work world as well. Interestingly, men's impulse to resist their assigned social role—angry, driven, compulsively hard-working—was given weight by medical science. Doctors noted that typical male behavior put men at serious risk of heart disease. "What had been defined as masculine maturity and understood as 'success' began to look... like a hazard to men's health," writes Ehrenreich.

The 1960s were a time of enormous social upheaval. The war in Vietnam tore at the nation's heart. The draft yanked men out of their lives and threw them down into the jungle to fight for their lives. During this era the male role polarized into extremes: long-haired freaks and hippies on one side, close-cropped hardhats on the other. It was a time of immense social experimentation, not just with drugs but with radical alternative lifestyles: free sex, communal living. The new generation threw out the values of the generation that had come before. All bets were off. Many observers have noted that the Baby Boom generation was the first to grow up under the threat of nuclear annihilation, which led them to realize that there may indeed be no tomorrow. Thus the question, "How shall we be men?" was answered, "Hey, man, just do your own thing."

Women saw that change was happening and that the time had come to liberate themselves from their own constricted social roles. They organized a movement to achieve their political and social goals. The change had been brewing for some time, ever since Betty Friedan's book *The Feminine Mystique* appeared in 1963. She identified some of the sources of women's problems in social forces such as advertising and psychoanalysis. The women's movement of the early 1970s, however, was more specific: the enemies were men—male chauvinist sexist pigs.

Some men saw that the changes women were demanding would actually benefit them by relieving some of the burdens of their own roles. Not surprisingly, however, other men felt very threatened by the loss of status and power (not to mention being labeled as "pigs"). They had already been branded as the "weaker sex," medically speaking; psychologists decried the male attitude as hopelessly rigid. The war in Vietnam, and the protests against it, reminded the world that male aggression could be a deadly force. The women's movement now eroded the traditional male image even further.

For men, the 1970s meant a period of adjustment. Some men sided with the women's movement and tried to shed their outmoded concepts of maleness entirely. Others tried to redefine yet again what it meant to be a man, hoping to find the right balance of male and female traits. Still others entrenched themselves even further into the classic male stance to defend themselves against the "castrating bitches" who threatened them. During this time the so-called human potential movement burgeoned, creating mass-marketed therapies, such as *est* and transcendental meditation, designed to help people get in touch with themselves and increase their awareness.

One problem faced by thousands of men, however, went virtually unnoticed. When soldiers returned from the lost cause of the Vietnam War, they were greeted not as heroes but as failures. The nation that had sent them to face the nightmare of jungle war now turned away. These men who suffered wounds of body and soul came home, only to find that their need for healing might never be met.

The men who had not gone to Vietnam were also angry and suffered inner conflicts about the position they had been forced to take.

Both groups experienced an overwhelming sense of victimization. Watergate also played a major role in men's loss of leadership, fueling personal feelings of vulnerability and powerlessness.

After three decades of social upheaval, men in the 1980s found themselves faced with a new range of options for being men. No longer was it expected, as it had been of their fathers, that they marry right out of school, settle down, find a job with long-term prospects and security, and raise a family. Instead, many men devoted extended periods of time to "finding themselves." A survey found that, in the mid-1980s, only a third of the population regarded unmarried men as "sick," compared to 53 percent a generation earlier. Many men chose to marry later, if at all, and often chose partners who wouldn't be a drain on them financially. Cohabitation became a more acceptable option. The government even invented a term, POSSLQ, to describe "persons of opposite sex sharing living quarters." One of the lasting images of this decade, which Tom Wolfe called the Me Decade, is the Yuppie, the young urban professional driven by greedy materialism. Barbara Ehrenreich summarized the path men had been following since World War II as "the flight from commitment."

Now, in the early years of the 1990s, things are changing again. The stock market crash of 1987, followed by the Persian Gulf War and a serious recession in 1991, ended the financial roller coaster ride. We entered the "New Age," a mushy amalgam of cosmic consciousness, environmental awareness, high technology, marketing savvy, and just plain trendiness. Comedians even identified a new group they dubbed SNAGs: "sensitive New Age guys." The Persian Gulf War, unlike the Vietnam War, restored the image of the soldier as hero. It also gave us our first female prisoners of war and the first women soldiers killed in action.

A NEW SOCIAL SCRIPT FOR MEN

What will history say of the changing roles of men in our own decade? How will society rewrite its script this time?

Will fathers refuse to give up access to their sons five minutes after they are born, as Robert Bly urges? Will men find ways to show their sons what their work is and what it means, which over the last 150 years they have forgotten how to do?

And what changes will be seen in men's relationships with women? As women achieve self-fulfillment through education or careers, they will be more complete and independent beings. Will men find in this trend an opportunity to shed some of their burden as breadwinners and protectors, and welcome a new sense of equality?

Will men learn to become more connected with each other, drawing on other men for strength, wisdom, and support? Will society teach men that their male traits— aggression, self-control, and so on—are of value at certain times but not at others? Will we take a lesson from our own love of sports, and realize that aggression and competitiveness may be needed on the job but must be turned off when we arrive at home? Will we go a step further and find that a more cooperative way of dealing with others at work is more satisfying and productive?

The answers are by no means clear. From our vantage point as therapists, we still see many men wrestling with problems that arise directly from the way they are being socialized, from the lessons they learn about becoming men.

If society can teach men to act out their natural aggression, it can also teach them ways to contain it. Men need to learn the difference between aggression, which means acting forcefully to meet one's needs, and assertion, which means stating one's needs clearly and positively. A man who says to his wife, "I need some T.L.C. right now," is being assertive; the one who grabs her breast and says, "Let's screw," is being aggressive (not to mention crude). We need to find ways to help men recognize and articulate their needs in healthy and constructive ways.

Men today are taught to be competitive. Athletes are the high-paid heroes of our day, the role models most boys look up to. Humans learned to be competitive when resources were scarce and the technology to use them limited. Today some nations and groups compete to achieve new heights of excellence, while others compete to see who can do the most damage to the planet. We need a new social understanding of competition. In a nation where resources are abundant, men need to learn that there are times when it's okay not to compete, that they will still be men. They need to hear the message that cooperation is not only possible, but desirable. The ability and the desire to work together is as much a part of human nature as competition.

Society teaches men they must be in control. The message has been that the more power they exert over themselves and others, the more successful they are. Here's one way this theme commonly shows up. A woman tries to open a pickle jar but finds it difficult. Without hesitating she gives it to the man to open. He twists it. Nothing happens. He bangs it on the kitchen counter. Still nothing. He runs it under hot water. He tries pliers. He considers every possibility but one: that he can't open it. The woman has learned that failure at a particular task doesn't mean she's a failure as a person. The man, however, sees his inability to open the jar as a sign that he is a weak and inferior person.

Men hide behind a kind of male armor to conceal the fact that they sometimes are not in control—that they, too, feel lonely or anxious or in need of help. We need to teach men a new message. Men must accept that it's okay at times to surrender control, to depend on someone else for help. We especially need to teach men to accept failure, to realize that lack of success does not mean that they are worthless human beings.

Many men have been taught that to be loved means to be needed. The more women need them, the more they feel loved. That's why so many men feel threatened by women who have been liberated from being dependent on others. We must help men learn to distinguish between love and need, and to realize that a loving and independent woman who is an equal partner can make for a better and more fulfilling relationship.

Society trains men to ignore their feelings, to suppress their pain, to neglect the signals that tell them they are hurt. To be a man means to be strong and invincible; to give in to pain is to surrender one's maleness. Too often, when men do express their feelings, they are criticized or told their feelings are somehow not acceptable. For the sake of health and survival, we have to change that message. We need to teach men that feelings are like a gauge on the car dashboard that signals when something is happening inside the engine. By learning to read those signals early on, men can exercise a little "preventive maintenance" and avoid an unnecessary breakdown.

Men have learned that being a father means providing for their families. Unfortunately, many men interpret that to mean providing just food and shelter. We need to help men realize that they can provide much more. As role models, they can play an equal role in the life of the family. They need to learn to make themselves available to their children, not just physically but emotionally. They must be open to their children's feelings and respond to them in a positive way, which can only happen if they learn to be emotionally responsive themselves. A father needs to provide not just bread on the table, but what Robert Bly calls a kind of "spiritual food" as well.

Society teaches men to base their identities on the work they do. We need a social revolution to change the nature of the workplace. We need less emphasis on hierarchy—who is up, who is down—and more on cooperation. We need businesses to recognize the need for greater flexibility in work scheduling, higher employee participation in the decisions that affect them, and more sensitivity to the needs of families. Companies need to implement "wellness programs" that provide for employee's health in areas of weight control, smoking, and physical health, as well as education about drug and alcohol abuse. By offering parental leave or time off to tend to sick relatives, companies may find they reap such rewards as greater employee loyalty, higher productivity, and less "down time" due to employee stress and on-the-job impairment.

Of course, many men, especially those in positions of power prefer to stay where they are. As long as they do so by choice, there's no problem. It's when men hold on to roles because of pressure from society that trouble starts. Here's an analogy: Someone removes the pin from a hand grenade and gives it to a man to hold. The man is told, "You are now Executive Vice-President in charge of hand grenade explosion prevention. We'll pay you $150,000 a year *not* to let go of that device." Great job, right? The guy's rich and powerful. But would you trade places with him? This little story illustrates a key point: True power lies in the freedom to choose and act on options.

SIGNS OF CHANGE

Obviously this new script for socialization will take an enormous effort on society's part. And the list of revisions we've suggested here is by no means complete.

Although we have a long way to go, we can see many signs of improvement. Gender-based treatment programs are contributing something to that process of change. The Men's Forum programs we sponsor, for example, both reflect and participate in this trend. Hopefully, as men participate in such programs and in other types of men's activities around the country, they will carry the message to other men. In time they will be a growing influence on the way men are socialized.

Men are learning to honor their maleness, not to be ashamed of it. They are claiming greater flexibility in their behavior and attitudes. They are learning to free themselves from the restricted roles imposed on them by the process of socialization and to discover newer, more satisfying roles: mentor, colleague, uncle, friend.

They are learning, too, that to be fully a man means to accept that they are made up of many parts. To be alive is to be plugged into a kind of psychic alternating current, where the transition between states—male and female, hard and soft, assertive and yielding, emotional and stoic—is necessary to provide life-sustaining energy. That energy is the *true* power of maleness.

Chapter 4

BODY AND SOUL:
PHYSICAL ASPECTS OF MALENESS

During his last argument with his wife, Jack got so furious he ripped the telephone out of the wall and hurled it through their bay window.

"Man, I just blew up," Jack said to the others in his therapy group. "I got the phone bill and saw how many calls she'd made, and I just lost it."

It wasn't his first violent outburst, but Jack's wife told him if he didn't get help it would be the last one she would watch.

"So now she's threatening to divorce me," he said. "She told me to come into treatment because I had to change. Hell, I can't change the way I was born. She doesn't understand the way guys are. But I don't think she'll be happy until I get my balls cut off and part of my brain dug out of my skull."

Over the next several weeks Jack learned a lot about "the way guys are." By the time he left the hospital he found there were in fact some important ways he could change—and still keep himself physically intact.

THE BIOLOGICAL BASIS OF MALENESS

Nature or nurture? Heredity or environment? Which is more powerful in shaping our personalities? In this book we discussed the power of socialization first, partly to suggest that our inborn traits are heavily influenced by culture. Human nature, in other words, is largely a product of human nurture. Men pick up many signals from their society about how to be a male. Those social lessons can change within a short time. Men get further confused when the roles they are taught to play seem at odds with the biological forces that drive their behavior.

As Jack's story shows, somewhere along the line he got

the idea that "it's okay for men to be violently angry because they are built that way." He couldn't understand why his wife hated his behavior and threatened to leave him unless he corrected it. What Jack needed to learn was that, yes, his biological maleness is a force to be reckoned with, even honored. But if he expects to be a successful, happy person, he needs to get control of his basic drives.

Jack wasn't far off when he identified those parts of the body where his maleness resided. Obviously, the testicles are the most male parts of his body.

But in some ways, a man's brain is also different from a woman's (although many of those differences can be overridden by social or personal change). By making such a claim we realize we are stepping onto a minefield. Any talk of physical gender differences (apart from the obvious differences in sex organs) sparks controversy. A lot of people would rather ignore the evidence that men and women are different in the ways they think and feel. They are afraid if we admit some gender differences are biologically fixed and not subject to social change, then discrimination based on sex can be justified. For example, women may be barred from taking jobs that require inborn "male" skills.

Masculinity and femininity are not purely social inventions, however. Biology may play less of a role in creating gender identity, but it plays a significant role nonetheless. It's fair to say that society builds on biology. Identifying gender differences doesn't mean we are claiming that one sex is superior to the other. But to shut our eyes to biological differences is to ignore reality.

THE BASICS

The most obvious physical difference between the sexes is that men's bodies are bigger. Primitive men, like other male mammals, had to be big and blustery if they expected to frighten off their enemies or, if that failed, to dominate them in battle. Human tribes whose men were puny or timid didn't last very long.

Males provide sperm to fertilize eggs and assure the survival of the species. Of course, sperm cells have quite a way to go before they reach their target. That's why males are made to penetrate females and deposit their seed. A man has to act if he wants to penetrate, so men are neurologically and chemically programmed to be the sexual aggressors. Survival of the species demands it.

Other differences: At birth, baby boys weigh an average

of one-half pound more than girls. Male infants' hearts and lungs are slightly bigger, although their livers are smaller. Symbolic of male impulsiveness, baby boys tend to be born sooner—there are more males among the shorter pregnancies and more females among the longer ones. (However, prematurity in a baby is defined by its weight. More girls are born at low weights, thus more are considered premature.)

As an adult, the average man is about five feet ten inches tall and weighs about 160 pounds; the average woman is about five feet three and weighs about 135 pounds. The average male brain is about 5 percent bigger than the average female brain, and the heart about 20 percent heavier. The man's volume of blood, as well as his lung capacity, is about 40 percent larger and he has about 20 percent greater skin surface area.

Men are also stronger. Physical strength is a product of body size, height, and muscle-to-fat ratio. In men, this ratio is about 43 percent muscle to 14 percent fat. Women's bodies are about 23 percent muscle and 25 percent fat. By age 17, males have about 50 percent more hand grip strength, arm-pulling strength, and arm-pushing strength. Women, however, tend to have more endurance; they are better insulated against cold and their higher fat ratio gives them deeper reserves of energy.

Another basic difference: Men's genitals are outside their bodies, women's inside. This arrangement makes men more defensive, because they want to protect their soft spots— not just the physical ones but the emotional ones as well. It also makes them more aggressive, since that's a good strategy for concealing vulnerability.

GENETICS

The genetic blending that produces a human being is an astounding process. One lucky sperm cell, possibly lured by a chemical substance produced by the egg, outswims its millions of rivals and penetrates the egg cell. Once inside it sheds its shell, and the genetic materials in both cells merge. This material weighs only two-millionths of a millionth of an ounce, but it contains all the codes necessary to create a human being, from eyebrows to toenails and everything in between.

Each cell in the body has a nucleus—a kind of command-and-control center. Inside that nucleus are 23 pairs of chromosomes. A chromosome is like a thread; strung along that thread, like tiny beads on a necklace, are the genes.

The genes are blueprints that carry instructions that the cells carry out to perform their jobs.

In women, all 23 pairs of chromosomes match. Men, however, are different. For them, only 22 pairs match—the last one doesn't. We describe that 23rd pair as "XY" to illustrate the mismatch. In women, that 23rd pair is called "XX."

Cells reproduce by dividing in half. When the nucleus splits, each new nucleus still ends up with the necessary 23 pairs of chromosomes. Each new cell in a woman's body thus continues to have the "XX" pattern. All men's cells split and carry the "XY" pattern—*except* the sperm cells. When those split, they carry *either* the X or the Y chromosome. Thus, in the game of genetic roulette, the one (and only) sperm cell that penetrates the egg determines the sex of the child-to-be. If that sperm carries the X chromosome, it will merge with the X chromosome of the egg cell to create an XX child—a female. If it contains the Y chromosome, the child will be XY—a male.*

That Y chromosome carries every piece of information necessary for the human body to develop into a male. In a way, females are the "default mode" of the species; all fetuses are female *unless* there's a Y chromosome to trigger maleness.

With their double X's, women have a kind of genetic backup system. If there's a slight defect in a gene strung along one thread of the X chromosome, the odds are very high that the matching gene on the other X will be perfect. This correct gene will usually be the one that governs the way the cell works; the instructions carried by the imperfect gene will be ignored.

Here's the problem: men don't have that backup system. If there's something wrong with their X chromosome, there's no matching X to fill in the genetic blank. All they have is a Y. For this reason, men are prone to experience a number of illnesses and other genetic defects that in most cases won't appear in women. We refer to these conditions as "X-linked disorders."

Because of this genetic vulnerability, males in many ways are truly the weaker sex. More males than females are

---

*Through rare genetic mishaps, some people carry unusual combinations of chromosomes: XO—that is, no second X chromosome; XYY—a male with an extra Y; and so on. These conditions lead to serious problems with development—XYY men are known to be extremely violent, for example—which we don't have space to discuss adequately here.

conceived in the womb—but more male fetuses die before coming to term. At four months' gestation, there are roughly two male stillbirths for every female. There are about 105 boy babies born for every 100 girls, but fewer boys survive their first year, so that the sex ratio becomes roughly even.

We know that certain conditions are X-linked and occur more frequently in men. Among these are color blindness, hemophilia, autism, dyslexia, stuttering, and a certain kind of muscular dystrophy. Men are more vulnerable to immunological disorders, including the condition in which the body fails to produce any defenses against infection whatsoever (as in the famous "Boy in the Bubble" story). Although all the facts aren't in, there are indications that other conditions may also be part of the hazards of being male. These include such disorders as certain types of alcoholism, learning disabilities, attention deficit-hyperactivity disorder, and so on. In our efforts to save the males, we must be aware that their physical heritage may predispose men to develop certain severe medical and emotional problems.

THE BRAIN

Many years ago a researcher dismissed the notion that there could be any differences between the brains of men and women. "Might as well speak of the female liver," this person commented.

However, as medical science becomes more precise, we are learning that, indeed, there may be important differences in areas we never thought to explore before. A recent study, for example, found that compared to women, men have a larger supply of the enzyme that breaks down alcohol in the stomach. Thus, as society has long suspected, some men may actually be better able to "hold their liquor" than some women. What other surprises lie ahead?

There is still a lot of research to be done on the human brain, and often one set of findings contradicts another. What follows must thus be read with some caution, since tomorrow's headlines may contradict what we're about to say.

Earlier we mentioned that men's brains tended to be larger than women's. Before you jump to conclusions, you should know that brain size has little to do with actual intelligence. Some geniuses have small brains, while some idiots have large ones. Bigger, in this case, does not mean better. Some reports suggest there are more geniuses among men, but there are more mentally retarded males as well.

More important than brain size is the way the brain is

organized. The brain is divided into two halves, called hemispheres. Evidence indicates that male and female brains are different in the way they are "lateralized"—that is, in the jobs for which the two hemispheres are responsible. Simply put, the left hemisphere handles the analytic stuff—particularly language—while the right hemisphere specializes in visual-spatial skills, the processing of emotions, and, perhaps, music.

The stereotype of the male is that he is better at analytical thinking while women are better at emotional thinking. If that is true, it may be because the man's left hemisphere is more powerful, while the right hemisphere is dominant in the woman. Is there evidence showing this is so? Yes. Scientists can record "heat maps" of the brain that indicate areas of activity in different colors. When a person speaks, has an emotion, or feels a sensation, a wave of color, such as red, can be seen flowing through the brain. Hot spots indicate the brain area that is primarily responsible for managing the signals. It turns out that language *does* generally get processed in the left hemisphere, while visual and spatial tasks are taken care of in the right. Some patterns of activity are different in men and women.

Another method is to study the brain function in a person whose "bridge" between the hemispheres, the corpus callosum, has been severed or who has lost part of the brain due to disease or trauma. Such studies show that women's brains tend to be more globally organized. That means a function such as language is spread across *both* hemispheres. In men, functions tend to be more localized in one half or the other.

If women are more globally lateralized, they need to have more connections between the two halves in order to process the information. But do they? There's an intriguing finding that suggests they do. You see, the hemispheres are connected by the corpus callosum, a fibrous band of tissue that carries nerve signals between the halves like a bridge. In women, the corpus callosum tends to be slightly thicker than in men, and contains more nerve fibers. This finding— highly controversial and not yet confirmed—suggests that women may be better able to process information from one hemisphere to the other.

Experiments also suggest that, because the halves of their brain work more independently, men may be better at handling several verbal and visual-spatial tasks simultaneously. Women, in contrast, appear to be better able to grasp the *connections* between events. The stereotype of women is that they are more sensitive to other people's needs and their relationships; the stereotype of men is that they are better at analyzing information from several sources at one time—watching TV, listening to their wives, and reading the paper, all at the same time. We may one day find these stereotypes are true because they come from basic structural differences in the way our brains are organized to function.

STRESS

Stress is anything that produces a change in the body's state or function. Stress can be good—having a baby, getting a promotion, winning the lottery—or bad—illness, getting fired, watching your house burn down.

When subjected to stress, the body kicks into high gear to lessen the impact. The fight-or-flight response is a stress reaction to help us recognize danger, redirect blood and energy (in the form of sugar) to the muscles, and prepare us either to act or to retreat. Much of this response is triggered by hormones released from the adrenal glands, including adrenaline (epinephrine) and cortisol. Cortisol reduces inflammation; by stepping up release of cortisol during stress, the body prepares to handle injury and pain. Stress also causes breathing, heart rates, and blood pressure to rise. Sweating increases to help cool off the system. Once the danger passes, other chemical messengers circulate, telling the body to settle down.

Today we don't have to fight off lions and tigers and bears. Modern stressors are long work hours, unnatural exposure to constant artificial light, environmental hazards, 24-hour access to news of the world's disasters, and the frustrations of daily life in a highly technological world. A little stress may be good, because it exercises the body systems and keeps them primed. Too much stress—well, you know what happens: The heart gives out, the immune system weakens, the muscles and joints suffer.

Men today are at risk because of the ways their bodies react to stress. A woman might be just as aggressive and competitive as a man, but her body handles the stress differently. Studies have found that women under stress don't show the same increase in heart rate and blood pressure as men. They produce lower levels of cortisol and epinephrine. This latter hormone causes blood to clot; less of it in circulation means women are better protected against heart failure.

If we hope to save the males, we need to do two things: We need to reduce the stress in men's lives as much as possible, and we need to train men to learn healthier ways of reacting to stress. Instead of throwing phones through windows, for example, Jack learned ways of talking to his wife and negotiating limits on the number and length of her calls. As we'll see in the third section of this book, there are other strategies that can also be effective.

HORMONES

In addition to regulating stress, hormones serve other functions, many of them gender-related.

Hormones are produced by glands of the endocrine system, such as the thyroid, the pituitary, and the gonads (ovaries in women, testicles in men). These chemicals travel in the bloodstream and affect virtually every cell in the body. Some hormones act directly on tissues; some work by triggering (or stopping) the release of still other hormones that actually do the job. There are dozens of hormones that control everything from height and weight to mood and metabolism. Because of the gender differences in the way people are "juiced," it stands to reason that brains of men and women are specialized in different ways to deal with the barrage of hormonal chemical messages.

Men are also governed by a different hormonal balance than women. Note that we didn't say different *hormones*, but a different hormonal *balance*. The distinction is crucial.

You may be surprised to learn that men's and women's bodies contain basically the same chemical ingredients. We classify some hormones as *androgens* ("man-creating hormones") and some as estrogens (from the word "estrus," meaning the female sexual cycle). Men have both androgens and estrogens, and so do women. The ratio of these chemicals is what is important.

Let's look at testosterone, the classic male hormone. Testosterone is produced by the testicles (in women, in much smaller amounts, by the ovaries). It is an anabolic steroid, which means it is used to build up proteins. When, at around age 12 or so, a gland in the brain called the hypothalamus matures, it releases certain hormones. These hormones in turn collect in a boy's testicles, building up for about a year. When the level of hormones reaches "critical mass," testosterone production begins and—*wham*—puberty happens. Testosterone makes the penis grow and the pubic hair sprout. Another hormone, FSH (for "follicle-stimulating hormone"), tells the testicles it's time to start making sperm.

Testosterone is associated with sexual drive, in women as well as men. In normal men, high levels of testosterone correlate with aggressive behavior, crime (especially violent crime), and responsiveness to threats. Studies on men born with an extra Y chromosome (XYY) find they tend to be even more impulsive, antisocial, and aggressive than normal men. Testosterone also enhances a person's persistence and attention, alleviates fatigue, and contributes to the "fight-or-flight" response.

One of the notable differences between men and women, and one that we must contend with in our psychiatric practice, is the fact that men are far more likely to display sexual deviation in the form of rape, exhibitionism, and sexual molestation of children. One approach to treating such cases is by using medications that block the effects of testosterone, which is another way of saying that testosterone may be involved in triggering these deviant behaviors.

Interestingly, testosterone appears to weaken the immune system. Women with low testosterone levels and men who have lost their testicles have fewer infections and are at lower risk of heart attacks. They also are more resistant to infantile diarrhea, childhood leukemia, Legionnaire's disease, and certain viruses. Here's some startling news: Castrated men also live longer.

Another key difference is that men's bodies constantly produce hormones at a fairly steady rate. Women, by contrast, produce hormones in cycles. The most obvious cycle is menstruation.

Woman's ovaries produce estrogens, a general term for the "feminizing hormones," and other hormones including progesterone. Evidence suggests estrogens promote a woman's sense of calmness and well-being. The female hormonal mixture makes biological sense. Women carry babies inside their bodies for nine months and nurse them for months afterward. It is appropriate, then, for women to be less governed by impulse, less hostile, and more in control of their sexual drive. These behaviors, like many others, are governed by the hormonal ebb and flow.

IS THERE A "BONDING HORMONE"?

Space doesn't allow us to discuss all aspects of hormones and their impact on development and behavior in men and women. Before we close, however, we want to mention a hormone that has caught science's eye. This hormone, called oxytocin, is produced by the pituitary gland in the brain and is most noted for its role in pregnancy, causing contractions of the uterus during labor and stimulating the flow of breast milk. (Many women in labor are given pitocin, the synthetic form of oxytocin, to help move childbirth along.)

Recently, however, scientists have found that oxytocin is active in both sexes, in humans and other animals as well. Its job, apparently, is to bring about happiness. How? By stimulating sexual interest and passionate response; by triggering the sensations of sexual arousal and orgasm (and post-coital satisfaction); even by triggering the urge to cuddle.

Oxytocin also apparently produces the feeling of joy when people interact—not just lovers, or parents and children, but friends, neighbors, and perhaps even strangers as well. We mention this because it is tantalizing to think that human interaction is biologically rewarded through a hormonally governed feeling of joy.

The implication for men is enormous. Some years ago, the noted anthropologist Lionel Tiger theorized that the closeness men can feel for each other—sometimes called "male bonding"—has a biological basis. He wrote that primitive men needed to form groups in order to hunt and suggested that such links became "programmed"—that is, part of our biology. A sociologist, Peter Filene, suggests that in order for men to be fully masculine, they may have to rediscover "the deep jostling warmth that male ties can provide."

Whether or not male bonding is a biological urge (mediated by oxytocin?) or merely a social one remains to be proved. The likeliest answer is that it is both. From our experience as therapists, however, we can state with certainty that modern men do not have enough opportunities to bond with each other. They are alienated from their fathers; they have lost sight of the importance of such roles as uncle, brother, mentor, or friend. For whatever reasons, biological or cultural, they don't have the same access to their emotional natures as women do, and they lack the vocabulary to express their feelings. If bonding is a basic urge, then our modern world has done men harm by attempting to eliminate it. The loss of bonding puts men at risk, emotionally and physically, by making them feel alienated, separate, and alone.

When men come together as men—whether informally or as part of a therapy group or men's weekend—and when they are not distracted by competition, one-upmanship, or chasing after women, a transformation happens. When they let down their masks and speak to each other from the heart, they experience a deep change. A string is plucked that resonates deep within their chests. They discover feelings they had long ago suppressed, but which now rise to greet them like a long-lost friend.

Men need each other. It is a biological fact. The only way we can save the males is by providing them the opportunity to be together, to grow together, and to understand together. We need to teach them how to make that happen. If we don't, men will continue to suffer the emotional and physical devastation that is described in the next section of this book.

Part II

MEN IN THE DANGER ZONE

Prologue

Echoes from the Talking Stick

The stick is passed from hand to hand. Chris takes it and speaks to the others in the circle.

"I feel close to you guys tonight," he says. "That's strange, because I'm so far apart from the other people in my life. My wife and I hardly talk any more. When we do talk we just get sore at each other. I work hard and the kids are with her all day. But when I come home they don't want to spend time with me. I don't have a lot of time to just hang out with the guys. I can get pretty lonely, even in a houseful of people. I feel sad a lot of the time, but a guy isn't supposed to let that show."

Jay is next. "Somewhere I guess I learned it wasn't right for me to tell someone I was angry or that I was hurting. So I drank to cover it up—'eighty-proof anesthesia,' I called it. But I knew if I could just keep drinking, sooner or later I'd get to a point where I could let it all out and no one would mind. 'Jay's just drunk again,' they'd say. 'Don't pay any attention.' It's as if most times I have to bottle myself up, but when I'm drunk I'm allowed to cry."

In Pete's hands, the stick vibrates with the memory of a distant battlefield. "I put my ass on the line for my country," Pete remembers. "I was told to walk into the jungle and kill everything that moved. I did some horrible things that I'll never forget, even though I'd give my left nut to forget them. I thought I was doing it to protect my family back home. I was lied to, man. I came back and found out no one believed in what I was doing, not even the people who gave the orders. I got sold out, and I don't think I can ever forgive the bastards who did it. Ever."

"When I was twelve," remembers Frank, "a neighbor down the street asked me to come and help her move some furniture. When we finished she gave me a Coke and told me to sit down on the couch and rest. She started feeling my crotch. I was so scared I couldn't move. I never thought it was possible for a gal to rape a guy, but she did. When I left she said, 'Now you can tell all your buddies you got lucky.' I didn't feel lucky. I felt like shit."

"I called my folks the other day to wish my dad happy birthday," says Bill. "I told him I was coming to this men's weekend. My dad said, 'What is that, a bunch of pansies sitting around whining about how bad they've got it?' For a moment I thought he was right and I almost didn't come. But then something hit me—that's the problem! I thought how all my life my father has been telling me I was doing everything wrong. I remember trying to come to him when something was bothering me—I wasn't doing good at school, I had trouble with a girlfriend. He'd tell me to work it out for myself or just 'be a man and take it.' If he'd been drinking he'd usually just haul off and belt me one. In a way coming here is like telling my father that I'm looking for something he never gave me, because he wasn't there for me when I needed him."

The next man takes the Talking Stick. He notices it is warm from the hands of those who have held it and from the energy they have given to it. He adds to it his warmth and the deep vibration of his voice before he passes it on....

Chapter 5

MEN AND DEPRESSION

In *Iron John*, Robert Bly speaks of the ways a man descends into the depths of his despair. Without such a descent a man cannot fully explore his pain and emerge again into the light a whole man. "Depression," he writes, "usually surprises us by its arrival and its departure. In depression, we refuse to go down, and so a hand comes up and pulls [us] down."

Bly is a poet, not a doctor, but he has captured the essence of the disabling medical condition called depression. Depression pulls us down into a world where feeling dies, where helplessness and hopelessness are the only features on a bleak landscape. The writer William Styron calls depression "darkness visible," and describes it as a "howling tempest in the brain." Another writer speaks of depression as "frozen tears."

We must be clear. Depression is a serious illness that can be treated medically. It is a different problem from "the blues," a temporary feeling of sadness that has a clear cause. Depression, in contrast, can last for months, even years, and can severely disrupt a person's ability to function.

Depression can also be lethal: Perhaps 15 percent of seriously depressed people commit suicide.

There are several types of depression. One type, called a major depressive episode, produces a low mood that, hopefully, returns to normal after a while. This is called unipolar depression, because mood changes occur in only one direction (one "pole"). Such episodes can recur, in some cases several times a year. Perhaps one in five people have a variation called dysthymia, a major depression that subsides only somewhat and persists for two years or more. The other main type is called bipolar depression, because it involves mood swings in two directions—from very high to very low and back again in an exhausting emotional roller-coaster ride. Sometimes people refer to this as manic depression. A variation on this is Seasonal Affective Disorder, or SAD, in which the person starts to feel depressed with the onset of winter and feels better with the return of spring.

Depression is often called the "common cold of psychiatric disorders." Nearly 10 million Americans experience depression in a six-month period.

Depression is usually thought of as a "woman's problem." There is some truth to that stereotype. Virtually every study on depression in modern countries reports that twice as many women as men experience unipolar depression. (About three times as many women as men have SAD, while the incidence of bipolar depression is roughly equal between the sexes.) Some studies find that perhaps one in four women will have a depressive episode, compared to one in ten men.

This ratio is somewhat misleading, however. It suggests that far fewer men than women fit the clinical picture of a depressed person. What we have found in our practice, however, is that more men are experiencing clinical depression than was suspected. In other words, perhaps the official description of depression isn't broad enough to include the "male" experience of the disorder.

Why should this be the case? There are several reasons. Depression is classified as a mood disorder. Women have long been known to be more sensitive to their moods. They are biologically programmed and socially reinforced to respond to emotional signals. It is "socially acceptable" for women to suffer from disturbed moods. When they do, they are more likely to show up in their doctor's office to get help, and the doctor is more likely to recognize the nature of their problem.

With men it's a different story. Remember the description of depression as "frozen tears." Men are often cut off from their feelings at an early age. One of our patients remarked that, at the age of 6, he was reluctant to bait a fishing hook with a worm or to clean the fish he had caught. Once, in the presence of his uncles and two brothers, the father upbraided the boy for his squeamishness. "I'm gonna start a 'no wimps club,'" he said, "and you're gonna join it." Our patient apparently learned his lesson: Several years later he was arrested for torturing and killing several neighborhood pets. No wimp, he. Later he sought help because he had withdrawn so far into a world of cold isolation. He was unable to form or maintain healthy relationships.

There are countless other examples of how men's feelings get cut off. A boy cries because he gets hurt during the soccer match and is humiliated by his coach or his father or his teammates. A mother tells her 8-year-old son not to get angry, saying, "For heaven's sake, one day you'll end up killing somebody with that temper." An adolescent struggling to deal with his raging hormones feels devastated at being rejected by a girl he loved. "Forget it," his well-meaning older brother tells him. "There are millions of women; if you've seen one, you've seen 'em all." To defend against future pain, the young man starts to see all women as objects—and treats them accordingly.

Thus men are taught to suppress their feelings. In time some men may become emotionally numb, unable to connect with other people or to derive pleasure from food or activities or even sex. This total lack of feeling is a key symptom of depression—and men are trained by society to develop that very trait!

Another reason depression is diagnosed more often in women is that they are more likely to seek treatment. Men, in contrast, will usually hold off seeing a doctor until the problem reaches a crisis point. And they are even more reluctant to seek help for an emotional problem. One patient remarked, "I wanted to come in a couple of months ago, but my father said that a *real* man wouldn't go crawling to a shrink. Men should either fix their problems themselves or just bear up. He made me feel doubly ashamed—once for being sick, once for wanting help." Men have to admit to being a failure in order to seek professional assistance.

One last point: depression in men often shows up in a disguise. In many cases a man who drinks, who uses drugs, who explodes in rages may be experiencing depression. Yet he copes with his troubled feelings in ways that are socially "acceptable." Our culture says it's basically okay, even kind of macho, for a man to go out and get drunk at a bar and maybe pick a fight and end up hurting somebody—or himself—very badly. It's *not* socially okay for him to say, "I'm in pain and I feel sad and I need help." If he does, he resigns his membership in the Fraternity of Macho.

SYMPTOMS OF DEPRESSION

Low Mood: This is the essence of depression. Many people feel "down in the dumps" because of some unfortunate event in their lives, but they usually snap back in a few days or can be cheered up. Depressed people feel low for long periods—at least two weeks, and sometimes up to nine months. Nothing anyone does will help them "snap out of it." You can't snap out of depression, any more than you can snap out of heart disease.

Helplessness and Hopelessness: These are the twin valleys of depression. Helplessness is the person's feeling that he can't do anything to make himself better. Hopelessness is an overwhelming sense of futility and despair, the feeling that the sickness will go on and on in an unrelieved infinity of pain. Many depressed people state it is this double-whammy of helplessness and hopelessness that causes them to think about—or even attempt—suicide.

Anxiety: Depression makes people feel something awful is about to happen. Coupled with low mood, anxiety sometimes causes depressed people to want to stay home and not face the world. People may feel anxiety as nervousness or fear.

Agitation: Many depressed people seem unable to sit still. They often pace, pick at their nails or skin, or, in severe cases, even beat their heads against the wall.

Guilt and Shame: Guilt relates to a specific event; shame relates to the whole person. When you feel guilty you believe that what you *did* was bad or wrong; when you feel shame you believe that *you* are wrong or bad. Depressed people often feel they have done something horribly wrong or are somehow responsible for their problem. They also feel that their illness makes them shameful in the eyes of other people. True, our society often does place an unfortunate stigma on people struggling with psychiatric disorders—as if the problem itself wasn't bad enough. Yet people with depression often feel that they are a disgrace to themselves and their families, a feeling that causes them to withdraw from society and, in some cases, to lose their will to live.

Low Self-esteem: Depression makes people feel they are worthless or terrible or shameful. They blame themselves for everything that happens, criticize themselves, and feel a sense of self-loathing. For men, inability to succeed at work or assume responsibility for supporting a family can produce intolerable feelings of low self-esteem.

Anger: One common description of depression states that it is "anger turned inward." People may be upset about their situation, but rather than "rock the boat" and cause trouble they direct their feelings inward. When they do, they aren't taking any steps to correct what's really bothering them. Anger turned inward may degenerate into depression, or may emerge as alcoholism, rage, or other troublesome problems.

Physical Symptoms: Depression is by no means "all in one's head." Headaches or stomachaches, even ulcers, can be common. Many depressed people have changes in sleep patterns, especially early morning wakening—their eyes flutter open at two, three, or four a.m., and they can't get back to sleep. In other cases—what we call "atypical depression" —people end up sleeping ten or twelve hours a night but wake up without feeling rested. Sleep disturbance is one of the worst symptoms of depression, since it robs people of energy and prevents them from thinking clearly.

Changes in eating habits are also common. Depressed people sometimes lose their sense of taste and appetite or lack the energy to eat properly. In atypical depression, people experience an increase in appetite. Depression often leads to weight changes, either because of the increase in appetite or as one of the direct effects of the illness on the body. (Weight gain can also be a troublesome side effect of many antidepressant medications.)

Loss of Pleasure and Drive: Depression robs the body of its appetite for food and sex. Depressed people slowly withdraw from the activities that formerly brought them pleasure. They stop seeing friends, give up their weekly racquetball games, cancel hunting trips. They pull back from family and friends, preferring to stay at home, alone, in their rooms.

Disturbed Thinking: Sometimes people with depression experience difficulty concentrating, remembering, or making decisions. They focus on the negative events and thoughts almost exclusively. They hear compliments but interpret them as insults; they can't see flowers, they only see the weeds. They dwell on thoughts of loss and failure, which only reinforces their sense of hopelessness.

Suicidal Thoughts or Actions: Perhaps the most alarming symptom is the preoccupation with death and suicide. *Suicidal ideas must be taken seriously.* As we noted, perhaps fifteen out of a hundred depressed people end up killing themselves. Often they will reveal their intentions in odd ways, such as saying "goodbye" instead of "goodnight" or giving away their possessions. Often a suicidal person will say something like, "You'll all be better off when I'm gone." A person who makes such remarks needs immediate help.

DIAGNOSIS

A physician who hears a patient say "I feel sad" and who then writes out a prescription for an antidepressant isn't doing the job. Good medical care requires a thorough examination before the diagnosis can be reached. Many physical ailments, such as a thyroid disorder or cancer, can cause symptoms of depression. The physician also needs to explore the patient's whole situation, asking probing questions about the patient's relationships, recent events such as divorce, relocation, or loss of a job, and so on. There is no lab test for depression; the best way for doctors to discover it is to talk to their patients.

TREATMENT

Depression can be treated. There are many approaches that have done millions of patients a world of good. Handled properly, between 80 and 90 percent of depressed people can get relief from their symptoms.

The bad news is, if you don't know how to ask for help you may not get it. And men, as we've said, are masters at keeping their need for help hidden. While many episodes of depression eventually lift on their own, they can still drag on for months. About half of the people who have one major depressive episode are at risk of experiencing another.

The most effective treatment, depending on the exact nature of the depression, often involves a combination of medication and psychotherapy. Over the last thirty years or so many effective antidepressants have come on the market. Among the main types are:

- Tricyclic antidepressants, such as amitriptyline (sold under the name Elavil) and imipramine (sold as Tofranil).
- MAO inhibitors, such as isocarboxazid (Marplan) and phenelzine (Nardil).
- Serotonin uptake inhibitors, such as fluoxetine (Prozac).
- Other types of antidepressants with unique mechanisms of action, including bupropion (Wellbutrin) and trazodone (Desyrel).
- Lithium, a highly effective medication for the treatment of bipolar disorder.

Each of these medications has a different combination of advantages and drawbacks. While most of them are about equally effective, each has its own pattern of side effects that may be more or less tolerable, depending on the person taking it. Typical side effects include weight gain, dry mouth, blurred vision, drowsiness, lowered blood pressure, and constipation. One complication is that three to six weeks may elapse before a person feels the effects of the medication. If one type of medication doesn't work, the doctor will usually change the dosage or switch to another type.

The decision to use medications depends on several factors. The people who invariably need antidepressants are those who are hopeless, helpless, almost completely dysfunctional, suicidal, and in need of hospitalization. Medications are also useful for patients who don't necessarily feel hopeless or helpless, but whose lives have been severely affected by their condition. Even mildly depressed people can benefit; once their symptoms abate, they are more able to look at their problem and work on solutions through other forms of therapy.

No pill can solve a person's troubled relationships, past emotional trauma, or unhealthy behavior. At best, medication will relieve the symptoms so the person can start working on these problems.

That's where psychotherapy comes in. Psychotherapy—what some call the "talking cure"—brings the patient and a trained professional together to work on ways of changing the patient's disruptive thoughts, feelings, and behavior. Psychotherapy is useful not just for depression, but for psychiatric and emotional problems ranging from substance abuse to post-traumatic stress disorder.

There are many different approaches psychotherapy can take:

- *Cognitive therapy* explores the troubled thought patterns that may be contributing to the problem.
- *Behavioral therapy* works to change the patient's behavior.
- *Interpersonal therapy* explores the patient's current social world and looks for trouble spots, such as in the marriage, within the family, or at work.
- *Psychodynamic therapy* explores the patient's past experiences and current reality to find the emotions and the unconscious motivations that may be driving the patient to act in certain ways.

These therapies are usually short-term, lasting around six months to a year or more if needed. Usually most depressed people do not need, nor will they necessarily benefit from, psychoanalysis, which is the long-term, lie-on-the-couch method most often used when a person wishes to achieve a fundamental change in personality.

THE GENDER-SPECIFIC APPROACH

There's one treatment strategy that hasn't yet made it into the textbooks. We are convinced, however, that it is extremely valuable. The strategy is to look at, and deal with, the problem from a gender-specific point of view.

Surprisingly, this simple but effective technique isn't widely used. Some therapists tend to look at patients simply as generic human beings. Ignoring the person's gender, however, is as foolish as ignoring other critical data, such as age or marital status. But when we take the man's maleness into account, we suddenly understand his problem from a vitally important perspective. Even better, we can talk to him in language that reaches him and that he can react to. Best of all, we can work out a course of treatment that, because it honors his maleness, stands a better chance of freeing him from his torment.

The surprising thing is that it took so long to discover this idea. For years therapists have seen the value of helping women deal with their problems in a gender-oriented way. Women must cope with enormous feelings of powerlessness in our society. They are often victims of violence, abuse, and rape, as well as more subtle forms of oppression: economic inequality, job discrimination, and so on. Women's gender roles contribute to their mental stress. Women have long benefited from treatment that focuses on their needs as women, not simply as "humans." Being in a room with a woman therapist, or in a group with other women, makes them feel safe. It gives them the opportunity to express themselves without feeling judged or criticized by men.

Why shouldn't the same principle apply to men?

In a men's program, patients develop a new awareness about the pressures in their lives. They can see how society creates roles for them and what happens when those roles are at odds with their own dreams and desires. They can learn that they have value as people, not just as breadwinners or warriors. They can discover how their "male training" is interfering with their ability to create and enjoy healthy relationships, not just with women but with other men as well.

We'll have much more to say about the gender-specific approach in the next section. We have touched on it here to indicate how a treatment program that focuses on men and their needs is of value in calming depression—the "howling tempest in the brain."

FROM THE FILES: LARRY

Meet Larry. Married eighteen years, two children. At the age of 45, he had worked for a truck-and-equipment rental company for nearly twenty years. Larry described himself as "pretty traditional." He had always been the breadwinner and, by mutual choice, his wife had never worked outside the home. Ten years ago Larry went through an alcoholism treatment program. He had been sober ever since, with the help of Alcoholics Anonymous (AA), a strong support network that he'd built up over the years, and some maintenance therapy at our clinic. At his job, he was delighted when he was promoted to manager. Six months later the company went belly-up. He immediately plunged into a depression.

In his clearer moments, Larry sensed that his company had "done him dirty." He had been loyal, had given his all, but the company jerked him around. More often, though, Larry blamed himself for the problem. "If I'd worked harder, been more efficient, maybe they wouldn't have failed," he said. He felt guilty and ashamed. He was a disappointment to his family, he said. He was afraid his kids would starve. "I can't look my girls in the eye anymore," he said. He mentioned that his wife wasn't too thrilled with his being in a men's therapy program. "I'll bet all you do is sit around and complain about women," she said.

During one session of a men's therapy group, a patient remarked that "one of the rules of our society is that men aren't allowed to fail." Larry's head jerked up. "You got that right," he said. "Right now I feel like the biggest fucking failure in the whole state of Texas. I let everybody down—my company, my wife, my kids, myself. I want a drink so bad I can taste it. So now I'm letting AA down, too."

Someone in the group made the point that, on the contrary, Larry's company had let him down. They had failed; he hadn't. He was merely paying the price. All his other concerns about letting people down followed from that fact. Larry nodded thoughtfully.

Partly because of his work in therapy, Larry mustered his resources and his self-confidence to begin looking for another job in earnest. At one point he panicked; a downturn in the economy was making it tough to find work at his same level. Meanwhile he felt that his wife was jumping on him, saying he wasn't trying hard enough and accusing him of not really wanting to be responsible. In the group Larry listed all he had done in his job search. He was surprised when the others declared how impressed they were. One patient said, "Man, you've sent out more résumés and made more phone calls in a week than I've done in my entire life." Gaining such a perspective bolstered Larry's self-esteem and enhanced his resolve to keep trying.

Some months passed, however, and Larry had had little luck. His money had just about run out; he had fallen off the wagon; his wife was making ominous threats about "a future without him." In therapy, Larry stated that he did have a job offer, but it meant a cut in salary and a step back in position. He felt that accepting the job would doom him forever. The others in the group rallied to his side. "You've gotta do what you gotta do," they said. Larry talked about his anger at his wife for pressuring him to succeed. "It's not your fault there are no jobs out there," someone said.

Larry accepted the job offer. Getting back to work has restored a great deal of his pride and self-esteem. He realizes this isn't his dream job, but it is "okay for now." He still has a sense of loss about his old company and his lower status. His greatest fear is that he'll never climb the ladder to an executive position. He's also been sober now for several months. Meanwhile he and his wife have worked out some of their problems. She now works part-time to supplement their income, and enjoys it. She still isn't totally convinced that he should stay in the men's program, but she has seen enough evidence of progress that she accepts his participation.

Larry is dreaming about starting his own business. The others in his therapy group have been supportive, offering encouragement not just in words but in practical advice and referrals for help. Recently Larry remarked, "Sitting in this room with you guys has made all the difference."

TAD

When Tad and Luanne came to the clinic, they were asked what their problem was. Tad, 48 years old, jerked his thumb toward his wife and said, "Ask her. She's the one who's bothered, not me." Luanne talked about how their relationship was eroding. "Tad doesn't talk to me," she said. "He's so silent and remote, like he's withdrawn from me. He just comes home and watches TV and falls asleep. He never does any work around the house. He never says he loves me. We've grown apart; we don't have anything in common. He never goes anywhere with the family or spends time with our two boys. I thought he may be having an affair. In any case, it seems like we're headed for a divorce."

When asked for his side of the story, Tad said merely, "If she says so."

After a few sessions of couples therapy, we discovered that Tad had some of the classic symptoms of depression. He had lost much of his interest in activities; he often felt anxious and agitated and had trouble sleeping; he felt guilty and ashamed about the situation. He had changed jobs many times, never feeling satisfied or happy. Most troubling was that he felt helpless to do anything to improve matters, and was hopeless that his future held any promise of happiness. Taking an antidepressant lifted his spirits, which confirmed the diagnosis. At that point we suggested that Tad come in on his own and take part in the men's program for a while.

Perhaps not so surprisingly, Tad found that being in a room with a male therapist and, later, a group of other men made it easier to open up about his situation. Tad spent a few group sessions just listening to the other men. It seemed like he was trying to pick up the habit of talking about what was happening inside him. Eventually he spoke up. He hadn't wanted to say anything bad about his wife when she was sitting next to him. "Part of it," he said, "was I'd feel kind of like a traitor. But part of it was I knew she'd use anything I said against me when we got home. Now, though, being with you guys, it seems safe to say some things and not worry about getting the silent treatment."

Tad said he didn't think their marriage was so bad. "It isn't a lot of fun," he commented, "but it doesn't seem much different from the way most of my friends are." He had agreed to come into treatment because Luanne wanted it. "I didn't care," he said, "I've given up. I didn't want any hassle. I hate fighting, and I usually don't have the energy to argue with her. I agreed to give it a shot, just to shut her up. I didn't expect anything out of it. I expected the therapist to just take her side and try to get me to be a better man. I was surprised when I found out the therapist wasn't blaming me, but was interested in what my view of this whole mess was."

Over time Tad identified what he thought was the main problem. He got married, he said, because everyone else he knew was married. He chose, not the love of his life, but the woman he was currently dating. Once married, he had to surrender his dream of being an architect and settle for being a housing subcontractor. He admitted he was uncommunicative with his wife. "When I get home after a tough day all I want is a little understanding. All I get is grief. We have nothing interesting to say to each other, and when we do say something it always gets misinterpreted. I just found it easier to keep my mouth shut. I never hit her, but I can see that there are some silent ways I can be abusive." He wasn't interested in other women; he wasn't interested in much, period. At first he said he still loved Luanne. When pressed to explore his feelings further, he said, "Maybe I don't really love her. I don't think I ever did. Now we just seem to tolerate each other. That isn't what I wanted out of life."

Tad found that, in therapy, he could safely explore his feelings without being criticized or contradicted. He began thinking about what his life would be like after a divorce. No one in the group ever told him what he should or shouldn't do, but they encouraged him to be honest with himself.

At one point he realized that his father had never been happy in his marriage, either. The father moped around the house, acting sullen and withdrawn. More often, he would stay away from the house entirely. He never took Tad fishing or hunting, never took him to ball games. Tad became aware that he had really missed that closeness with his father. In one session he cried; he had suddenly remembered that at age

15 or so he had sworn he would never do to his children what his father had done to him. "And now look at me," he said. "I'm following in his footsteps, but I'm walking on the wrong path."

Tad got something from the men's group he never got from his dad: support, advice, feedback, encouragement. The men cared enough to listen to him and respond.

In the end, Tad and Luanne decided to get a divorce. It has been hard, but in his therapy he is working through those problems. He claims he is a better father after the divorce than he ever was before it; without feeling that his wife is standing nearby waiting to criticize him, he can be much freer with his sons. He has formed and nurtured friendships with men. He no longer tries to get all his emotional needs met through one relationship.

He is tentatively building a new relationship with a woman. He is working on being more open and expressive with her, and finding that she responds to that. "Maybe," said Tad, "this is what love is supposed to feel like."

STEVEN

For some months Steven's wife had been worried. Her husband, a 52-year-old bank vice-president, seemed to be brooding, edgy, and withdrawn. One night he woke up gasping for breath, his heart pounding. The sheets were soaked with sweat. The next morning Steven's doctor realized he was in bad emotional shape, and referred him to our clinic.

During the admission interview Steven spoke in a flat, monotonous voice. He muttered that his situation was hopeless, that nothing would change, that he was helpless to exercise any control over his life. "I want to die," he said evenly. Asked if he had made plans to kill himself he said, "No, I just don't want to live anymore." We asked how he would commit the act. He said, "I might overdose on pills or gas myself. Yesterday I was going to sit in the garage with the engine running, but I chickened out. I have a gun and I might use that."

Within the hour we admitted Steven to the hospital. If he hadn't agreed to go, he would have been committed by the courts as a danger to himself.

His diagnosis: severe depression with suicidality.

For several days Steven would barely talk or respond. No one could get through to him. He expressed no emotion, neither laughter nor sadness. Then, during a conversation with a therapist, Steven remarked that no one should bother treating him because he didn't want to live. "Why?" the therapist asked. There was a tense pause. Finally, in a choked voice, he said, "Because I'm a thief." It was as if the word caught in his throat like a fishbone. "I am ashamed, I hate myself, and I don't deserve to live." He eventually told his story: in order to get enough money to pay his mother's nursing home bill, he had rigged the computers at his bank to delay crediting deposits to customers' accounts, and had the accruing interest transferred to his own savings. "It was just pennies," he said, "but it was millions of pennies."

Steven's confession was a turning point. Gradually his whole story emerged. As a teenager he had been sexually abused by an older male cousin over a period of years. Frightened at the thought of being gay, and as if to prove his masculinity, Steven joined the military and was shipped off to Vietnam. There he saw plenty of action. To deal with his fears, he became deeply religious.

One day half the men in his charge died in an ambush. He felt an overwhelming guilt over the fact that he had survived while the men he was supposed to lead had not. The next day he was ordered to file a report in which the incident was depicted as a "major victory" for the Americans, with dozens of Viet Cong killed or wounded. Steven felt a knot tighten in his chest.

After returning to "the world"—the States—Steven was angry that the veterans had never been welcomed home. He developed what is known as a sense of entitlement: "The sons of bitches owe me."

Over time his bitterness gnawed away at him. He developed severe, incapacitating headaches and had two heart attacks. He had a quick temper and would lash out at anyone who spoke against the war in Vietnam. He married, but soon afterward lost interest in sexual relations with his wife. At one point he said that sex was "unclean and immoral." Eventually he became impotent. He blamed everything on his experiences during the war.

His bank crime grew out of his sense that he had been cheated by the world, especially by his commanders in the military. He had been so righteous and moral, however, that his crime sickened him—literally. His guilt and shame contributed to his many problems, including his suicidal feelings.

His treatment was long and sometimes difficult. His next breakthrough came when he made an emotional connection with the other veterans on the men's unit at the hospital. They immediately understood his feelings of betrayal and anger. In group sessions he spoke painfully about being sexually abused. He was startled when, instead of sneering or laughing at him, the other men expressed concern and told their own stories of trauma. He had no idea that other men had dealt with similar issues, and had thought he was the only person in the world with such a guilty secret. When at last he spoke of his recent crime, again he felt nothing but support. The other veterans, while they didn't admire his actions, understood his feeling of being "owed." Other men spoke of their own entanglements with the law and gave him hope that he could survive the ordeal. During this time Steven began to realize there were ways he could make restitution. The others offered suggestions.

Steven was in the hospital for two months. Finally his condition stabilized and, no longer suicidal, he was released. He continued taking medication and took part in outpatient men's group therapy sessions. He went to the authorities and confessed his crime; of course he was fired. Taking his psychiatric treatment into consideration, the court was lenient, giving him a suspended sentence and ordering him to return the money and perform community service.

In the men's group, Steven says he thinks his experience with the law enabled him to let go of his anger and his sense of entitlement. No longer does he feel that he has been deprived; instead, he feels the court gave him justice in the form of a reprieve. He is working on rebuilding his relationship with his wife and is trying to rediscover the pleasures of sexual contact and emotional intimacy. He is reaching out to form a support network with friends, other veterans, and "graduates" from the therapy program.

His greatest joy, he says, comes from the court-ordered community service. He works with the local veterans' hospital, conducting rap sessions and other programs. For the first time in years, he says, he is able to get out of himself and help others. "My story," he remarked, "is helping other people deal with their stories."

Chapter 6

MEN, SUBSTANCE ABUSE, AND ADDICTION

After three months at sea, the cargo boat makes for home port. For Jason, a 36-year-old shipboard mechanic, the trip has been a rough one—not because of choppy water but because it has been, for him, another three-month drinking binge.

As soon as his wife Maria spots him, she knows there's trouble...again. She can read the story in his bloodshot eyes and his haggard face. "You promised," she says, her mouth tightening. "You *promised.*"

"I know," Jason says. "Never again, I swear."

That night Jason goes to the local AA meeting. "I'm Jason," he says, "and I'm an alcoholic."

"Hi, Jason," the others chorus.

"I was here a couple of months ago," he continues. "At that time I'd had thirty-four days of sobriety. The day after the meeting I went back on the boat. I managed to stay sober for another week, but after a while I couldn't hold out. Everyone else was drinking—there just isn't anything else to do. I lost sight of myself, and stayed lost for the rest of the trip. I came here tonight to get back in touch with my Higher Power."

Two weeks later Jason is back on board ship for another cargo run. For a few days he sticks to his promise: no booze. Then one of the crew passes by his cabin.

"Sure you don't want a little snort, Jace...?"

THE BIG PICTURE

The use of chemicals to alter one's state of mind is as old as the human race itself. For thousands of years people have used plants, bark, roots, and fermented or distilled beverages to induce visions, to numb pain, to communicate with the gods, or simply to take themselves out of this world for a while. Society has made alcohol an integral part of every ritual, from weddings to funerals, from sporting events to ship-naming ceremonies.

Our society has decided that certain drugs—alcohol, caffeine, nicotine—are acceptable, while others—cocaine, marijuana, heroin—are not. The wonders of modern science have taught us to believe that all of our problems, from a runny nose to birth control, can be solved by popping a pill. Of course, a dose of aspirin might relieve a headache. But if it doesn't, if our problems are deeper than merely throbbing temples, the temptation is to reach for something stronger. For people who live in constant pain, physical or emotional, their need for relief is overwhelming.

There is a fine line between substance use and substance abuse. Perhaps two out of three Americans drink alcohol; most of them manage to do so in moderation and suffer no serious long-term effects. But over seven million people in this country are problem drinkers: their use of alcohol causes trouble for themselves or others in their lives. Another ten million are actually addicted to alcohol. Millions more are hooked on marijuana, cocaine, or other substances. Robert Bly calls the addictive state "the fastest growing state" in the country.

The misuse of alcohol, cigarettes, and drugs, legal and illegal, is the leading cause of preventable illness, disability, and death in this country. Alcoholism alone costs the country nearly $90 billion a year due to the expense of treatment, reduced productivity, property damage, and death. Drug abuse adds nearly $47 billion to that total. According to a report from the Research Triangle Institute, the costs of substance abuse are four times that of cancer and 33 percent greater than cardiovascular disease.

There are some encouraging signs. Consumption of beer and wine has been dropping for some years, and use of distilled liquors is down to its lowest point in thirty years. Government-ordered warning labels appear on every liquor bottle, and cautions to pregnant women are posted in every bar. "Happy Hours" are harder to find, and the national emphasis on fitness has made drinking and smoking less acceptable than it was.

Nonetheless, as therapists in a clinic and a hospital that offer substance abuse treatment, we sometimes feel we are on the front lines in the battle against substance abuse. Some people come to us because they realize they are sinking; others are dragged in by those who love them; still others come only because they are ordered by the courts or by their employers to get help or get lost. We've dealt with hundreds of people who have been pretty badly bruised by their fight against chemical dependency.

Most of these people are men. Because of the way they are brought up, because of the way their bodies are made, because of the pressures they face simply due to their gender, men are at special risk of chemical abuse. If we hope to save the males, we must understand this fact. More importantly, we must understand what to do about it.

JASON'S STORY: CHAPTER 2

The journey ends; the boat docks at the port. As Jason strides down the pier, he is surprised Maria isn't there to meet him as usual. After all, three months is a long time to be away.

He arrives home. With a shock, he sees that the house is empty: stripped of furniture, no signs of life. A note taped to the wall reads, "You're on your own. I can't live with a drunk. You didn't shape up so I shipped out. Maria."

Jason's first impulse is to smash his fist through a wall. His second is to cry. His third—the one he acts on—is to head for the nearest bar.

ALCOHOL

There are between two to five times as many male heavy drinkers as there are female. Most drinking problems first show up between the ages of 20 and 40. Alcoholism tends to run in families. Part of the reason for this is genetic; parents can pass on a susceptibility to alcoholism. The other part is social; alcoholic families act in ways that can lead to drinking behavior in the next generation. If Daddy's a drunk, and his response to stress is to drink, then Junior is likely to learn that drinking is an acceptable solution for him, too. Even if Junior elects to not drink, the disease can skip a generation and show up in a grandson.

In the past, alcoholics were thought of as lazy, depraved, or immoral people with no self-control. Now, science has shown that alcoholism is a progressive disease. Alcoholics need treatment, not condemnation. Society doesn't stigmatize people with heart conditions; it shouldn't stigmatize people with a drinking problem, either.

The earlier a person starts abusing alcohol, the worse the

problem can be. An adolescent who drinks heavily can become an alcoholic in six to eighteen months. People who start drinking as adults, however, might go fifteen years before developing the disease.

One of the worst symptoms of the disease of alcohol abuse is that it blinds people to its presence. Alcoholics are notorious for denying that they are in trouble. (A supposedly funny T-shirt reads, "I don't have a drinking problem. I drink, I get drunk, I fall down—no problem.")

The sad thing is, denial seems to be contagious. The spouse or family of an alcoholic will go to great lengths to deny the problem themselves. "John isn't a drunk, he just likes a few beers." "Daddy's tired this morning so he can't drive me to football practice." This tendency to deny the problem, and thus enable it to continue, is known as codependency. The word refers to the fact that the entire family is organized around the substance abuser's behavior. In some families, when you take away the abuse problem, the family loses its focus. It no longer has the main thing that holds it together.

A problem drinker shows denial when he compares himself to other drinkers. "I'm not an alcoholic," he says. "Alkies get the DTs; I've never had a hallucination in my life." Or, "I only drink on weekends, so I'm not an alcoholic." The truth is, alcoholism takes many different forms: daily intoxication; drinking large amounts at certain times, usually weekends; or long drinking binges followed by periods of sobriety. A person can be an alcoholic whether he drinks one beer or two six-packs or, for that matter, none at all. Part of treatment involves educating people about the illness. Once they know the facts, it's harder for them to deny the reality.

For male alcoholics, denial is a kind of double jeopardy. Men are masters at denying their feelings, especially feelings of pain or shame. It's hard enough for a guy to admit that he needs help with fixing a lawn mower, let alone with fixing his life. Coupled with the shameful stigma that society still attaches to alcoholism, a man is likely to deny his problem until it reaches a crisis point.

Unfortunately, it usually does. Alcoholics will usually persist in their behavior until their lives completely fall apart. Recent studies show that some residual impairment from even minimal use of alcohol can persist for up to a week following consumption. In other words, a few beers downed by a kid on a Saturday night can make it more difficult for him to take that test the next Friday morning. A man who drinks may become less and less able to function at his job. If he's an accountant, that can mean losing track of a few thousand dollars; if he's a drill press operator, that can mean losing a finger—or even a life. Drunken driving leads to the loss of thousands of lives and causes enormous pain and suffering.

Prolonged drinking contributes to depression, memory loss, and the inability to think or reason or follow simple directions. Alcohol damages the liver, the brain, the nerve cells, the stomach, the blood system. Chronic alcohol dependence increases the risk and severity of heart disease, pneumonia, tuberculosis, and neurological disorders. Some intriguing research suggests that alcohol destroys the hormones needed to trigger release of the body's own painkillers. Alcoholics thus may need to keep drinking in order to numb themselves to the pain, which their bodies had previously handled naturally.

Families suffer tremendously, too. Children witness their parents fighting or lying sprawled in a drunken stupor on the couch. Many times these children are forced to grow up too quickly, learning to compensate for their incapacitated parents by preparing the family meals or walking to their piano lessons or making excuses for why Daddy couldn't come to watch his son's softball game. Alcoholism contributes to financial ruin, separation, divorce.

In many cases, men get caught in a vicious circle. They are under the gun to perform as breadwinners, as providers and protectors. The pressure can lead them to seek relief in a beer or two. In time they may think they need a "quick one" at lunch to make it through the rest of the afternoon. They may stop off after work to hoist a few with their buddies. Eventually they become conditioned to using alcohol to relieve any stress—after a fight with the wife, after hearing bad news, good news, whatever. As their drinking continues and their ability declines, they may have more trouble on the job, leading to more pressure and more drinking. If not stopped, the cycle—or, more accurately, the downward spiral—leads to addiction and disaster.

Recently, our society has taken important steps to break the cycle. The word is spreading that alcoholism is a disease, not a moral deficiency. Research is helping doctors and the public understand the disease more completely, and the ability to help alcoholics change their behavior through sound medical treatment has improved enormously. The success of Twelve Step programs such as Alcoholics Anonymous has made a huge difference in millions of lives. Employers, concerned about people as well as profits, have set up programs to help workers and their families cope with substance abuse. Many of the patients we see come to us through referrals from such programs.

In short, the picture is changing. Today we are even able to treat codependency.

TOBACCO

For years the face of the Marlboro Man—rugged, tough, handsome—has glowered down from billboards and peered out from between the covers of magazines. The ad campaign effectively communicates its message: smoking is cool. Smoking is manly.

Men seem to get the message. Nearly 30 percent of men today are smokers, while only 23.8 percent of women are.

A report from the Surgeon General confirmed that nicotine compares with heroin or morphine in its addictive power. Despite this and other warnings, nearly 50 million Americans continue to light up every day. Each year, over 300,000 of those people will die from use of tobacco products.

WOODY

Recently we treated a patient named Woody at our hospital. Woody is black, 65 years old, and was a three-pack-a-day smoker. He had some serious problems. His wife died ten years ago. Six years ago, Woody finished his shift at an auto plant and picked up his paycheck. Inside the envelope was a pink slip; the plant was closing, and that was the first anyone had heard about it. He was devastated. He had worked there for over twenty years, had devoted himself "body and soul" to the place. "And this was the thanks I got," he said.

For several years, Woody, alone and jobless, did little besides sit around the house and watch TV. "Why should I go out?" he said. "I got no place to go, I got nothing to do." His children, all grown, became concerned. In retrospect, it was clear Woody was depressed. Then it hit him: a massive heart attack. He recovered, but became even more withdrawn. His ability to function lessened with each day. He continued smoking heavily. His children tried to get him to stop. "This is the one pleasure I have left," he said, "and you want to take it away from me." He didn't believe them when they said they loved and respected him and wanted him to live. To put a stop to their "nagging," as he called it, he stopped calling them and sometimes even refused to open the door to them. All for the sake of his smokes.

The children talked to our hospital staff and said they were concerned for their father, mostly about his smoking. They knew, however, that he'd never agree to get treatment for that problem. We suggested they try to convince him that what he really needed was treatment for his depression. Once in the hospital, we could address all of his problems. Reluctantly, Woody agreed to get help for his "case of the blues," as he put it. After admission, he was admitted to the men's program.

At first Woody refused to take part in the group sessions. "I know I smoke, but I'm not a drug addict like some of you," he said. "I'm a widower so I don't have trouble with my wife like I hear some of you say. I don't belong here," he said. The other men respected his decision not to speak in the sessions. But outside, when they'd pass him in the hall or spot him in the cafeteria, they'd greet him heartily and clap him on the back.

One day another patient said to him, "You know why you're here, don't you?" Woody said, "Yeah, because my kids say I'm depressed." "No, man, that's not it," the other man replied. "You're here because your kids love you. They're worried, and they want you to be around for a couple more years. Otherwise who are they gonna give any grief to?" Woody chuckled, in spite of himself. That was a turning point.

The next day Woody opened up a little and spoke to the group. Over time his story emerged. "After I got fired," he said, "I felt worthless, like an old newspaper. I was so ashamed that I didn't even tell my family for a week—just kept pretending to go to work. When that paycheck didn't come, though, they were bound to find out. That's when I got depressed and started smoking real heavy. I felt like shit, and I didn't care if I died. I knew I'd lost the respect of my kids, and that was hardest to take. I couldn't tell them how I felt. Hell, all I am is an out-of-work wrench turner. Most of them, they've got college degrees and jobs and families. What do they have to respect about me?"

Some of the other men pointed out that if his children were successful, it was because he had brought them up right and he could take pride in that fact. Woody seemed to brighten at that remark. Over the next few weeks he unburdened himself about his tremendous feelings of shame.

By the time he graduated from therapy, Woody had come to be known as "grand old man" of the group. In the safety of the therapy room, the other men had given him the power to confront his feelings and express them for the first time. He said he had learned how to listen to what his children were saying, and could now accept that maybe they did love him after all.

On his last day, Woody said goodbye. "When I came in here," he said, "I had three sons. Now I feel like I have twenty-five of them."

Woody even managed to stop smoking.

ILLEGAL DRUGS

For several decades our society tolerated, even extolled, the use of drugs. Everyone from rock stars to athletes to members of Congress used drugs and lived to tell the tale. According to the National Institute on Drug Abuse, by 1985, over 70 million Americans—a third of the nation—had tried illegal drugs.

As drug use became more accepted, the country's drug habit changed. In the 1970s, cocaine was used openly in nightclubs and dance halls. A "dose" of coke was the amount that could fit in a fingernail or a doll-sized spoon. By the 1980s a dose was a line, several times the volume of the coke spoon. People often went on binges, snorting an entire gram in one session. Similarly, due to improved breeding, the marijuana that people were smoking in the '70s and '80s was perhaps *thirty times* as potent as what the hippies smoked during the 1960s.

The drug scene changed again in the mid-'80s, with the arrival of smokable cocaine—"crack." Crack gives users an intense rush within seconds of inhalation. More of the active drug reaches the brain when it is inhaled than when it is snorted. So quick-acting and potent is the crack high that many people describe it as a full-body orgasm. The pleasurable feeling causes people to crave another hit, and another. Soon they are addicted and will do anything to get more drug—steal, abandon their families, even kill.

Today, anyone with a couple of hundred dollars' worth of lab equipment can manufacture a whole line of "designer drugs," including crack cocaine, "ecstasy," synthetic heroin, and smokable methamphetamine. There are some encouraging signs, however, that drug use is tapering off. As families and neighborhoods realize the havoc that drugs cause, as former users and rock stars rally to save the younger kids from self-destruction, society is becoming less tolerant of drug use. States create "drug-free school zones," where drug crimes incur automatic and stiffer penalties than elsewhere. A number of antidrug programs have proved fairly effective at deterring drug use and helping young people say no to drugs. Nonetheless, many millions of people continue to seek and use illegal drugs, with enormous cost in lives, health, and social stability.

The impact of illicit drug use hits both men and women hard. Women, tragically, seem especially drawn to crack. Doctors are treating huge numbers of women for diseases they contracted while trading sex for drugs. Crack-smoking women can pass their addiction along to the baby developing in the uterus. There is new evidence that men's use and addiction to cocaine also adversely affect child development. For years hospitals have dealt with rising numbers of babies born addicted to cocaine. Schools are now contending with a new generation of children born to addicted mothers and who experience severe learning and social disabilities. Women have trouble finding treatment centers that will accept them, especially if they are mothers, because there are no provisions for dealing with their children.

Men experience their own pattern of drug-related problems. Consider marijuana, for example. Boys and girls between the ages of 12 and 17 are equally likely to try marijuana for the first time. But between 18 and 25, pot smokers are 50 percent more likely to be males. We know, too, that alcohol and marijuana, even tobacco, act as "gateway drugs"; a youngster who smokes pot, for example, is highly likely to progress to harder drugs. The gateway concept is no mere "scare story" promoted by frightened parents; it is a scientific fact.

Marijuana affects hormones in both men and women. In males, pot lowers testosterone levels. It also causes sperm count to drop by as much as 70 percent in some patients. In some cases this low count persists even after marijuana use stops, thus lowering fertility permanently. Pot impairs short-term memory, concentration, and the ability to process information. People who smoke at school or on the job can't learn new material or carry out complex operations. Marijuana can lead to rapid heartbeat and elevated blood pressure. It also interferes with psychosocial development. Marijuana smoke contains cancer-causing elements, and because it is held in the lungs longer than tobacco smoke, one joint can be as carcinogenic as a pack of cigarettes.

Cocaine is a huge temptation, especially on payday. Ernie, a patient at our clinic, said that on Friday he would run from the office to his dealer, who, like a banker, gladly cashed his check and paid him in crack vials. On Saturday night, after he had smoked away his dough, Ernie would scrounge around for items to hock, even stealing from his girlfriend or his parents if he had to. One businessman, a realtor, said he sold off his buildings, floor by floor, to pay for his habit.

One particular concern about crack use by men is that the drug can trigger outbursts of devastating violence. Crack smokers become irritable and suspicious. They develop a very short fuse and will lash out at another person at the slightest provocation. In the past, violence associated with drug use was often seen during withdrawal, after the effects of heroin, for example, had worn off. Today, these outbursts occur *while the user is high*.

That's one reason there are so many reports of random shootings and fierce street fights in our cities. Nearly half of the cocaine users responding to a survey conducted by the 1-800-COCAINE helpline admitted that they had committed violent crimes or aggressive acts, and two-thirds of those said they did so while high, as compared to when they were coming down from the high. Of those violent acts, 25 percent were violent arguments; 20 percent physical fights; 13 percent robberies; 7 percent domestic violence. Other crimes included child abuse, rape, even murder. One out of six reported that their cocaine habit had led to them to carry a gun. Over 80 percent of crack users believed that crack caused their violent behavior. In some cities, over half the people arrested have traces of cocaine in their urine. Because cocaine is eliminated from the body quickly, this means that they had used the drug a short time before their arrest.

Like hemlines, drugs rise and fall in popularity. Now, in the early 1990s, heroin seems to be making a comeback. One reason is that people discovered that manic high of cocaine or amphetamine could be controlled by a snort or a shot of heroin. Newer, more potent forms of natural and synthetic heroin have also hit the streets. There are perhaps half a million heroin addicts in the country; drug officials fear the number is on the rise. Heroin injection requires needles; addicts often share needles to reduce the cost, which increase the risk of AIDS and other diseases.

Other drugs include hallucinogens such as LSD and phencyclidine (PCP or "angel dust"). Some people abuse prescription medications, including tranquilizers and sleeping pills. Recently there has been concern about a powerful form of smokable methamphetamine, called "ice," which produces an immediate high that lasts for up to eight hours.

Drug use threatens not just men, but our whole society.

JASON'S STORY: CHAPTER 3

When Jason came to the clinic for help, he was, as he put it, at "low tide." His wife had left him. He had tried to "work his program" through AA, but was unable to stay sober while trapped and isolated on a boat for months on end.

As we talked to Jason, we learned more about his history. His parents had essentially written him off years ago. Although Jason was obviously very bright, in school he had trouble keeping up his grades. Branded a failure, he fell in with the wrong crowd and turned to using drugs and alcohol. Since he couldn't live up to his parent's expectations, he found a group whose expectations he *could* meet. It wasn't long before a brush with the law placed him on juvenile probation.

Since he believed education held no future for him, he joined the military right out of high school. In Vietnam he trained as a mechanic. His unit was placed in the line of fire but never got to take part in any action. He drank heavily to pass the time and to relieve the boredom and the tension.

Back stateside, he took the job on the boat. It paid well for someone of his educational level. Besides, there was no place in the middle of the ocean for him to spend his money. The only thing there was to do was—drink.

In the clinic, Jason's test results revealed that he had a learning disability. His IQ was quite high, but he had trouble putting together information in sequence. It became clear that this disability made it hard for him to learn and apply new information, such as the principles taught in AA. The problem had also disrupted his career in school and set him on the wrong path. The tragedy was not the disability; the tragedy was that no one had spotted the problem and helped Jason overcome it.

In therapy, we not only treated his addiction, we focused on Jason's roles as a son, as a husband, as a breadwinner. We untangled his feelings about being branded a failure by his parents and how that had led to his dropping out of school and enlisting in the military. "If I was a loser," he said, "the jungle was a great place to get lost." We explored his relationship with his wife and how being away for months had taken its toll. "I thought I was providing for her the best way I knew how," he said. "There aren't too many opportunities for a high school dropout to make thirty-five grand a year." He also saw how his choice of jobs had its downside: the boredom and isolation that fueled his long-standing alcohol addiction.

Jason felt that the others in his men's group understood his situation, recognized that he was not to blame, and offered him love and support in his search for solutions.

At the end of his course of treatment, Jason made the decision to quit his job on the boat. No one in his group suggested he take such an action; he came to that realization on his own. But the men supported his decision.

Jason worked with a state agency to find related work that wouldn't require him to be away from shore—and his AA support network—for more than a day or two. He's making less money, but he no longer feels like he is throwing himself away for the sake of a paycheck. He hasn't found a woman to share his life yet, but, he says, "You meet a lot more women on shore than you do in the middle of the Atlantic ocean."

The road to recovery is as long as life, but we think we might have helped save this male.

Chapter 7

MEN AND POST-TRAUMATIC STRESS DISORDER

Crawling on his belly, Nick inched along the narrow tunnel. He didn't dare use his flashlight. Instead he probed the ground ahead with his knife. Sweat dripped into his eyes. The smell of dank clay mixed with the smell of his own fear. He was stripped to his shorts so that his skin could feel any booby-trap wires strung along the cave. His every nerve was on fire.

In Vietnam, the enemy might be anywhere—in a tree, behind a bush, even in a hole. When the Viet Cong went underground, it was the tunnel rat's job to go in and dig them out.

Nick was one of the rats.

Suddenly he stopped. There was movement ahead. He thought he heard breathing. Just my own, he told himself. He wriggled forward again, but froze again when he heard a slight scraping noise. Taking a chance, he turned on his flashlight.

Shining out of the darkness ahead he saw the fierce gleaming eyes of a cobra.

Nick whipped out his .22 and plugged the beast. After confirming that no VC remained in the tunnel, he backed out, dragging the nine-foot carcass of the snake with him, hoping to take its skin as a souvenir.

He was eager to give the all-clear to his squad. As he reached the mouth of the tunnel he looked up—straight into the eyes of a Viet Cong soldier. His squad had been ambushed. The VC stuck a pistol into the tunnel—and shot and shot and shot and shot.

Nick backed up and pressed himself against the tunnel wall. He squeezed his eyes shut, waiting to feel the bullet that would take him out. He stayed there for what seemed like an eternity....

Nick was eventually rescued. He stayed in 'Nam another six months, clearing out dozens of tunnels and saving the lives of uncounted American soldiers.

Years later, however, back in "the world," his ordeal continued. Nick had frequent nightmares about snakes and tunnels and guns. He often woke up screaming and drenched in sweat. If he heard a car backfire, he jumped. Nick drank a six-pack of beer practically every night "to drown the demon," as he put it.

In January 1991, the night the Persian Gulf War began, Nick watched the coverage on television. The sight of missiles launching and guns firing, the sounds of explosions and military leaders giving orders, sent Nick reeling back in time twenty years. The odor of gunpowder burned again in his nostrils. Every emotion, every fear he had felt crawling in the tunnels came back to him, as real as now. It was too much. Nick broke down.

When his wife brought him to the hospital for treatment, the diagnosis was clear: post-traumatic stress disorder.

PTSD: A CLEAR AND PRESENT DANGER

In the mid-1980s, the American Psychiatric Association officially declared post-traumatic stress disorder (PTSD) to be a real illness. Such a step meant that medicine had finally recognized what survivors of severe emotional trauma have known all along: surviving a disaster, whether man-made or an "act of God," can have a permanent, devastating impact on the body and on the mind. It also helped the effort to save the males, since now many men have a label for their suffering and are entitled to medical treatment that is covered by insurance. They are no longer powerless over the nightmare that haunts them.

The recognition of PTSD was largely the result of the fact that thousands of Vietnam veterans needed treatment for psychiatric problems following the end of the war. Between 700,000 and 800,000 of the 3.5 million men and women who served in that conflict experienced PTSD serious enough to disrupt their lives and require treatment. Thousands more have experienced at least some of the symptoms of the disorder. PTSD is the sixth most frequent diagnosis at Veterans Administration outpatient facilities. The number of PTSD cases associated with service in Vietnam has risen each year. This increase shows that the public—and doctors—have become more aware of the problem, and that more veterans are willing to seek help.

Studies have found that the more intense the combat experience, the more severe the stress. Some skeptics have suggested that PTSD is "all in the head." They feel that people who claim to be victims of the disorder are using their experience as an excuse to be lazy or to withdraw from their obligations, or that they were "shirkers" or "weaklings" long before being drafted to fight the war. However, solid scientific evidence has shown that many sufferers of PTSD were perfectly normal, well-functioning human beings before they experienced trauma. Our patient Nick, for example, was a bright, successful, popular student, a varsity athlete, and a dedicated, patriotic soldier.

Of course, PTSD is a problem not just for Vietnam veterans. Perhaps three out of ten of the veterans now being treated for the condition were in combat in World War II, Korea, even Panama or Grenada. As this is being written, it is too early to predict how the Persian Gulf War affected those who fought there. The war was over quickly, casualties were light, and the returning soldiers were given a heroes' welcome, all of which should certainly lessen the burden. Nonetheless, in the months after the war, the media were filled with reports of the problems soldiers were having as they returned to their spouses, their families, and their jobs. It is impossible to know at this point what the long-term effects will be.

But trauma can come in many forms, not just war. Victims of earthquakes, hurricanes, and airplane crashes can have PTSD. Children who experience physical or emotional abuse, women who suffer rape, hostages or other victims of crime can all develop some or all of the symptoms. Children from alcoholic homes may suffer intense trauma. Losing a job or struggling through an illness or bitter divorce can produce signs of stress; these may require medical attention but are not, strictly speaking, symptoms of PTSD.

Many women have served valiantly in our armed forces, most recently in the Gulf, but they are still forbidden by Congress to take part in combat. Our emphasis in this chapter will be on post-traumatic stress arising directly from men's gender-related social roles—whether as soldiers, leaders, or family providers.

THE SYMPTOMS OF PTSD

Recent research shows that severe emotional shock is not just "all in the head." An overwhelming event such as war or natural disaster causes a huge increase in the body's biochemical activity. Chemical messengers flood the brain circuits, trying to carry information about the threat to the body and promote action to reduce the danger. Hormones circulate to control organ function and regulate stress. If the trauma is great enough, it can lead to long-term changes in brain tissue and other organs, causing the body to react as if severe stress were continually present even long after the situation has cleared up.

The psychiatrist's "bible," the *Diagnostic and Statistical Manual, Third Edition, Revised,* states that symptoms of PTSD arise following a distressing event that is "outside the range of usual human experience." Among these events are:

- A serious threat to life or health
- A serious threat or harm to children, spouse, family, friends
- Sudden destruction of the home or community
- Witnessing an accident or injury to another person
- Hearing distressing news about harm or threats of harm to a loved one

Such shocks would affect virtually all who survived them, no matter how brave or psychologically prepared they may be. Usually, symptoms don't appear during the stressful event, such as during prolonged captivity in a prisoner-of-war camp. Instead, symptoms emerge afterward, from several months to several years later.

In Chapter 1 we met Allan, who survived an explosion at a petroleum refinery. Many of our PTSD patients hold jobs in the chemical and manufacturing industries. They put their lives on the line during every minute of their shifts, dealing with dangerous materials or balky equipment. Their daily stress can be enormous. If you pile a disaster, such as an explosion or accident, on top of their already precarious load, you'll see symptoms of PTSD develop.

Nor need the shock always result from the unexpected. We recently dealt with a man named Jerry who had been an emergency medical technician for twelve years. He loved his job—it was exciting, dramatic, and unpredictable. He liked helping people and felt that he was doing some good in the world. Recently, though, he went out on a call and was the first to arrive at an accident scene. A man was trapped inside a badly mangled car. Jerry struggled to remove him, but could not. He tried to administer oxygen through a broken window but was unable to reach the victim, who soon died. Months after the event, Jerry had a breakdown. In therapy he revealed that he felt responsible for the man's death. He had been dealing for so long with other people's tragedies and pain, "breathing it in like air," he said. "I guess it had to come back to haunt me sooner or later." In his case, PTSD was the result of his having chosen a high-stress occupation—not a sudden accidental shock but a prolonged, self-inflicted wound. We focused on helping him deal with his feelings of hopelessness, and sense of guilt, and are happy to report that Jerry is back on the job.

The characteristic feature of PTSD is that people re-experience the traumatic event. As they do, they relive the intense feelings of fear, terror, and helplessness. They are suddenly flooded with intense, vivid memories that carry with them all the emotions and feelings of the original event.

Many times, PTSD victims have flashbacks, where they become convinced they are actually reliving or rewitnessing the experience. Psychiatrists refer to this as a "dissociative state." In such a state, people may appear to be sleepwalking or operating on a kind of "remote control." During a flashback, Nick, for example, would sometimes crawl under his bed as if it were an enemy tunnel.

Nightmares are a common symptom, especially those in which the dreadful scene is replayed over and over. Nightmares shatter sleep because they usually cause the dreamer to awaken. Many PTSD victims develop severe insomnia. They are afraid of falling asleep because they know the dreams will come again.

People with PTSD often experience repeated bouts of sudden, overwhelming emotions—grief, anger, and fear—for no apparent reason. Nick told us he might be walking down the street when, without warning, he is flooded with sadness. He feels his throat tighten and must fight to hold back tears. "People look at me like I'm nuts," he says, "a grown man crying on a street corner. Maybe in a way I *am* nuts."

PTSD causes people to avoid situations, sometimes without any apparent reason. They will withdraw emotionally, refusing to get close to family or friends. Obviously, for men, whom our society teaches to be emotionally distant and not to express their feelings, PTSD can make the situation worse. The disorder can cause people to swing between being emotionally numb and being overwhelmed by their feelings. Families often describe their member with PTSD as being cold, distant, preoccupied, or bored. Naturally, families are hurt when their loved one withdraws from them or just "goes through the motions" during their activities.

People who have had a severe shock will avoid anything that may remind them of what happened. Although many ex-GIs have found the Vietnam Veterans Memorial in Washington to be a source of healing, some veterans refuse to visit it, saying the sight of so many names of the dead would hurt too much. Victims of the Holocaust have experienced flashbacks when they see people in uniform or World War II documentaries on television.

If the disorder isn't treated, PTSD victims may spend much of their time avoiding people and places for fear that anything might trigger a flashback. Similarly, victims may avoid taking on new responsibility because they feel somehow responsible for the traumatic event. Typically a veteran will accuse himself of not saving the men whom he saw killed or wounded. Avoiding responsibility may translate into trouble holding or performing on a job, disturbed relationships with family and friends, or difficulty making or following through on decisions.

A common symptom is sudden irritability or explosive anger. We know, of course, that some men tend to be angry anyway, partly because of their basic instincts and partly because they are socialized to believe that anger is an acceptable emotion. Once they've made some progress in treatment, many of our PTSD patients realize that their anger stems directly from the feeling that they were "sold out" by their country, or exploited by bosses or leaders, or that they were made to carry out stupid, pointless orders.

Not surprisingly, PTSD patients report having trouble concentrating or remembering information.

As Nick's story shows, trauma victims sometimes startle easily, overreacting to sudden loud noises. Many people with PTSD have panic attacks, which produce rapid heartbeat, fast breathing, dizziness, nausea, and sweaty palms.

In Chapter 4 we described Steven, who felt horribly guilty that he survived an enemy ambush while others under his leadership died. Such survivor's guilt is commonly seen in PTSD. A Holocaust survivor may feel, for example, that his true place is in the grave with his parents. Some soldiers in Vietnam were forced to participate in horrific actions which, though probably necessary for survival in wartime, violated their sensibilities as civilized men. Other acts were senseless. "I stuck my bayonet in a five-year-old's gut," one patient told us. "I don't deserve to be alive right now."

Often such feelings as guilt, shame, sadness, and worthlessness appear in the form of clinical depression. One way to think about depression is that it represents an unfinished (or unbegun) process of grief. Unless the person recognizes the need to grieve—or even that there is something to grieve over—those unresolved feelings may continue to direct his life.

In many cases PTSD victims turn to alcohol or drug use as a way of coping with their pain. It is often the problem of chemical dependency that brings a case of PTSD to medical attention. A treatment program that is gender-oriented is more likely to uncover the underlying traumatic stress that may explain why the man succumbed to addiction.

TREATMENT

We have to identify our enemy before we can defeat it. The one positive thing about having PTSD recognized as a diagnosis is that we can focus on effective ways of treating it. Fortunately, experience with thousands of PTSD cases across the country over the last several years has shown that treatment does work to relieve and counteract the long-term effects of trauma.

The techniques for treating PTSD are, in a way, no different from those used in any other psychiatric problem. Individual, family, and group therapy can all play a part, depending on the person's needs and situation. The difference is that therapy concentrates on discovering the source of the trauma (usually not too difficult), recognizing the impact it has had, and dealing with the specific ways the problem has affected a person's life.

A PTSD victim is living in a kind of "twilight zone" between the past and the present, between the person he was before the event and the person he is now. In war, for example, a man who may have been a loving father or devoted husband is suddenly told to charge in and wipe out whole towns. Before he can kill the enemy, he may first have to "kill" part of himself. After the war, he must face the fact that he destroyed something inside himself, his respect for life, that was dear to him. If he can't accept that fact, he must bury the memory far down in his psyche.

Psychotherapy is designed to help people bring these conflicts to the surface where they can be explored and resolved. Some therapy techniques help people regain their sense of self-worth and their feelings of control over their emotions and their lives. Talking with therapists or other people in a group restores perspective and may help patients see that they are not personally accountable for a tragic event, but rather are victims themselves.

Family therapy helps because trauma victims often refuse to connect with others emotionally or physically. Family members need to learn about the disorder in order to help their loved one make it through the crisis and support him in his time of need. They may also have some issues themselves that therapy can help them resolve, such as resentment about the patient's emotional coldness or fear for their own safety. PTSD victims sometimes lose their desire or their ability to communicate with other people; family therapy can reopen those lines of communication. Everyone can also benefit by learning ways to reduce and manage stress.

In some cases of PTSD, medications can help. They won't necessarily cure the disorder, but they can help reduce some of its symptoms, such as anxiety or depression. We don't yet have a medication that relieves the symptoms of avoidance, such as alienation or emotional numbness.

Some studies suggest that certain antidepressants may be useful in treating PTSD. Lithium, commonly used in bipolar disorders ("manic depression"), has helped patients get control of their rage and their mood swings. Tranquilizers such as Valium (the brand name of diazepam) help calm people down during crises, but may be addictive. Heart medications such as clonidine, usually used for blood pressure, can help reduce such symptoms as violent dreams, instrusive thoughts, and explosive emotional outbursts.

Group therapy is invaluable. Sitting in a room with others who may have been through exactly the same situation is a powerful experience. It helps victims realize they are not alone, that others have not only "been there" but have survived. Through groups, people often shed their feeling that they are somehow responsible for the event and learn they need not feel unworthy or guilty. Many patients say they feel "confirmed" by their experience in group therapy: they learn that what happened to them was real, that their suffering is indeed something that needs attention, and that, despite what happened to them, they are valuable people who deserve happiness and love.

Therapy groups made up of men only are especially helpful. Without women present, men feel freer to discuss their fears and their pain. They don't have to worry about looking like "wimps" if they cry or talk about how scared they were during the trauma. They aren't distracted by the subtle sexual competition that may arise in a mixed group. Also, for many women, trauma means rape or domestic violence. Some survivors of such abuse tend to perceive all men as "perpetrators." Such a perception throws the process out of balance and prevents true therapy from taking place. The most important aspect of a gender-specific therapy group, though, is the fact that men can communicate with each other most easily in their own language. When a man says, "I was in 'Nam," and he sees other men nodding in empathy, he knows that they understand his suffering.

In other words, it's important to look at men in treatment with "gender glasses" on. In our program we take the patient's maleness into account and build our therapy around that. Men tend to have trouble recognizing and voicing their feelings anyway; if they are trauma victims, it may be very difficult for them to express what's going on inside. Men may need to learn first what their feelings are, and second that having feelings is okay. If therapists understand that, then they can find ways to communicate with men that are more likely to reach them. Most of all the therapist must create a safe environment, which is easier to do in an all-male therapy group. "Safe" means safe from criticism, denial, contradiction, or ridicule. We try to honor the fact that men have experiences that set them apart from women, and that they deserve respect for that.

Stories like the following suggest that such an approach is well worth taking.

SCOTT

For nearly fifteen years Scott had smoked a couple of joints of marijuana at night. He walked around in what he called a "blue haze," always slightly buzzed from the pot.

Most of the time Scott, a 40-year-old technician for an electronics company, seemed pretty laid back. Every so often, however, he would lash out in a furious rage. His second wife, Laura, described such moments as "like that scene in the movie *Alien,* where that creature bursts out of the guy's chest." It took very little to trigger Scott's explosions. One day, for example, Scott was struggling to fix the bathroom faucet. He didn't have much luck. Finally he got so frustrated he tore the whole vanity out of the wall and smashed it to bits.

Understandably frightened, Laura demanded that Scott get treatment or she would leave him. She blamed pot for "messing up his mind." Scott said he was sorry—he always said he was sorry—but Laura was firm: Get help or it's goodbye. Scott had been down this road before; his first wife had said the same thing, and had followed through with her threat.

Scott loved his wife and his stepdaughter, and didn't want to lose them. He was admitted to our program for treatment of marijuana use and possible depression. We also knew we would explore the reasons for his massive rage attacks.

In our interviews with Scott and during his therapy sessions, his full story emerged. He came from a very normal background; his parents, still living, had been married forever. There was no history of depression, substance abuse, sexual abuse, none of the past traumas we typically hear about. As Scott put it, "real *Leave It to Beaver* stuff."

A few years after high school Scott was drafted and thrown into the jungle of Vietnam as a combat infantryman. Most of the men he was with smoked the strong local pot to relieve their tension and terror. It wasn't long before Scott started smoking, too.

For six months he witnessed one living nightmare after another—burnt villages, shattered bodies. One day he was ordered to set some explosive booby traps. He did his job well. The next morning he returned to the site and was forced to look at the half-dozen enemy soldiers wounded and writhing in pain as a result of his handiwork. He never forgot the sight, nor could he forget, despite all his combat training, that he had inflicted pain on other human beings.

Eventually Scott was transferred to a new position as a door gunner on a helicopter. Out of the bush, Scott no longer had to focus on the rigors of day-to-day survival. Now he had hot meals and could sleep in a cot, not on the jungle floor. But he also had lots of idle time on his hands. He smoked even more dope. He had been taught by the Army not to become friends with other soldiers. He made friends anyway, only to hear that his friends had been shot down, blown up by a mine, or destroyed by enemy booby traps.

After his tour of duty, Scott came back to the States. When he got off the plane in San Francisco, he was heckled by war protestors, one of whom spit on him. "I felt too numb to even react," Scott remembers. "I guess when you've had mortars and those rockets we called flying telephone poles drop on you, you can put up with a little spit on your shoulder."

He tried to live at his parent's home in Florida, but had trouble readjusting. At night, the noise of street traffic kept him awake. When he did finally drop off, he'd wake again hours later, disoriented, not certain where he was, dripping with sweat. He continued smoking pot heavily, although he knew it made his parents furious.

He decided it was time to find himself. Having promised to devote himself to the Lord if he survived the war, he enrolled in a Bible college. "But I got burned out on the routine," he said. "All that praying.... After getting shot at, I thought I wanted a little quiet, but not that much." When his fellow students asked about his experiences in the war, Scott shrugged them off. In fact, he hardly mentioned those years to anybody. After quitting school, he picked up his pot habit again, very heavily—as if to make up for lost time.

He took a string of undemanding jobs, but didn't make much of any opportunity that came along. He couldn't stand taking orders from anyone. When a boss reprimanded him or criticized him in any way, Scott would lose control. More than once he went on a rampage, smashing company property or kicking over chairs. "You'd better grow up, man," one boss told him as he fired him. His parents rescued him from jail after Scott had started a barroom brawl, but told him they never wanted to hear from him again.

Meanwhile his nightmares continued. In his dream he saw the same human bodies explode dozens of times, always the same way. He smoked joints to keep himself "vegged out," as he put it.

He married. After a few years, however, Scott had pretty much "checked out." He showed no interest in sex, let alone hobbies or doing things with friends. His wife split, fed up with his drugs and his rage and his emotional withdrawal. He found a job with a consumer electronics company where he could work without much supervision, and managed to stay at it for a long period.

He fell in love with and married Laura, an energetic woman who ran her own graphics design business. She was very special, as was her daughter by a previous husband. Scott knew he loved them very much, but was frustrated that he couldn't "feel the feeling." He continued smoking pot, hoping, he said, to get in touch with himself.

Over the past two years Scott's rage attacks increased in frequency. He broke dishes, kicked dents in his car, and got into shouting matches if someone cut in line at the movie theatre. For Laura, though, smashing the vanity was the last straw. She demanded that he give up pot or lose her. Scott remembers a frightening moment when he told himself, I'd rather have the dope.

In treatment, Scott met other men who had been through the war. For the first time in years he talked about his experiences. "My parents were just horrified and didn't want to think their Sonny Boy could do such things," Scott said. "A lot of other people reacted the same way. If you weren't 'in country' [that is, Vietnam], you'll never understand." Now in the treatment program, however, he felt it was safe to open up. When he talked about setting the booby trap, another man said, "I hear you." That was all he said, but something resonated for Scott. He looked at the other man, and a bond of understanding formed between them.

During his stay, Scott was able to connect the threads of his life. He saw how his drug habit emerged out of a nightmarish situation. Pot alone hadn't messed up his mind; Vietnam had started the process. He saw, too, how he had clung to his habit because he had never dealt with the pain of his experiences during the war.

The turning point came when he realized that his anger came from his deep sense that he had been exploited and abused by his commanding officers. "They lied, they made us do things no human being should do, they abandoned us," he said. "We came back home but were treated like shit. People spit on me and called me 'baby-killer.' Not once did the leaders stand up for us and defend what we had done. What else can you do at that point but question everything yourself?" Scott saw how he had been unable to hold a job because he resented anyone in authority. Even his religious training made him angry at God, whom he called "Big Boss." By understanding the source of his anger, he was at last able to address it.

He learned, too, that his marijuana use had essentially arrested his emotional development. He went into the army at 19—not a boy, not yet a man. By wreathing his brain in a fog of pot smoke, he lowered his ability to learn from his experiences and adapt to circumstances. It became clear to him that the drug now threatened to ruin what little he had built up in his life.

As he graduated from the program, he told the other men, "I've been straight now for four weeks, the longest drug-free time since I shipped out. I smoked my first day in 'Nam, and it's been in my lungs ever since—until now. I feel like for the first time I might have literally gotten it all out of my system. The smoke has really cleared, in both senses of the term.

"It surprised me to know I could feel anything without pot, but talking with you guys and listening to you guys proved that I could. I can't swear I'll never be angry again, but knowing why I'm angry puts me in position of control. I feel like you've given me power over myself, and I like that feeling."

Scott's life has changed enormously and he has stayed off pot for over eight months. That's partly due to the fact that continued drug use was primarily a symptom of his fundamental problem—PTSD. He has also discovered deep reserves of emotional commitment to his wife, and for the first time feels like a father with his stepdaughter.

Six months after leaving the program, Scott reconciled with his parents. His mother came to visit and to meet her daughter-in-law for the first time. After a few days she was amazed at the change she noticed in her son. "Scott, you seem so comfortable with yourself," she said. "It seems like you've finally come home."

For Scott, at that moment, the war at last was over.

Chapter 8

MEN AND ANGER, RAGE, AND VIOLENCE*

EXHIBIT A: GARY

The car in front of him was taking its own sweet time. Move it, you old fart, Gary thought to himself. As Gary approached the intersection, the light turned red. Damn it, he muttered, I never make this light. He sat, fingers drumming on the steering wheel, waiting for the light to change. It seemed to take forever. Come on, come on, thought Gary, inching the car forward. Then the light did something odd—it started flashing. The car in front hesitated and Gary almost rammed him. He slammed on the brakes and blasted the horn. Meanwhile the other cars crept tentatively through the intersection. Get out of my way! Gary screamed. Finally the other car nudged its way through. As Gary started to move, the light stopped flashing and went back to solid red. He was stuck again.

As Gary remembers it, at that moment his mind filled with a red haze. With a howl of pure rage, he reared back and kicked the dashboard of his car furiously. He kicked and kicked again, destroying it utterly. A few moments later the red haze lifted. Gary blinked. His first thought was, what happened? His next was, oh, Christ, I've done it again.

NOTE: The authors are indebted to Newton Hightower, a therapist affiliated with the Men's Forum who specializes in the treatment of anger, for some of the insight, terms, and examples used in this chapter.

EXHIBIT B: MARK

Mark worked as an insurance claims adjustor. One afternoon the medical lab on the floor below his had a chemical spill, forcing the evacuation of the building. He came home early and found his wife in bed with another man. Mark told him calmly to leave the house.

A few hours later Mark and his wife sat on the couch. "What should we do?" she asked. "It's up to you," he said in an even voice, adding, "Do you love him?" "I think so," she said. "Then maybe you should go to him." "Is that what you want?" she asked. "I want what's best," he replied. "For you or me?" "For both of us."

His wife then asked, "What do *you* want?" Mark sat for a moment, staring at his hands. "I think I'll go to bed now," he said.

Two men: Gary and Mark. The question is, which of these men has a problem with anger?

The answer: They both do.

THE MALE VOLCANO

Men are raised to believe that anger is the only socially acceptable emotion they can have. We train young boys to push aside or swallow most of their feelings. Often, the only emotional option left to them which is sanctioned by society is anger. Anger can erupt in many ways, often as rage and violent behavior. Fighting and lashing out are "acceptable" in men. In his book *Why Men Are the Way They Are,* Warren Farrell describes this as the "male volcano."

Farrell also cites the findings of an interesting scientific experiment. Some groups of observers were shown a 9-month-old infant who was crying its little lungs out. One group was told the child was a boy; the other was told it was a girl. They were then asked to state why they thought the child was crying. The "girl" group said it was because she was afraid. The "boy" group, however, said it was because he was angry. Same behavior—but two totally different gender-biased responses.

It may be helpful to define some terms. By anger we mean an intense feeling of displeasure or hostility. The word anger comes from the Greek term for "strangle." That's appropriate; many angry people describe the feeling as a tightness, even a choking.

Rage is anger translated into action, usually violence of furious intensity. The word comes from the Latin meaning "madness" or "to rave," and is even related to "rabies." No wonder people who rage are sometimes called "mad dogs."

Violence is physical force intended to damage or abuse. Thus the equation: anger (feeling) leads to rage (action) and violence (damage).

The violence is of greatest concern, since it threatens other people. Today the problem of physical abuse—child abuse, wife abuse, rape—is enormous and tragic. Depending on the study, some researchers estimate that perhaps as many as one out of every six marriages involves wife abuse. Sexual violence is the quintessential male crime. According to some sources, one in four women can expect to be raped. In a strange way, rape is the way some men try to express power when they feel most powerless. Sex becomes a weapon, a way of inflicting psychic as well as physical wounds.

Without making too much of this, we should note that there is a positive side to anger. It is a very real part of human nature, bred into us over thousands of years as an important part of our evolutionary survival kit. Anger is the body's way of telling us that something wrong has happened, or that a problem has occurred that requires action to fix. Anger can lead to a resolution of a conflict, ideally without any major long-term damage. Someone who has been mugged or who loses a job because the plant closes without warning has a *right* to feel angry.

It is tempting for people to believe that all anger is destructive and should be obliterated. Life would probably be a lot safer, if a lot duller, were that to happen. The concern, though, is that ignoring a basic biological feeling such as anger would be more destructive in the long run.

If we want to save the males, we need to honor their fundamental maleness—including the anger. That doesn't mean we should encourage men to go around angry all the time or to lash out at the least provocation, like Gary. Of course not. What we need instead is a society that recognizes and accepts anger as part of the human spectrum of emotions and trains its members in the *appropriate* ways of handling and expressing that emotion.

Otherwise, as Robert Bly observes in *Iron John,* we risk creating a race of "naive men." He means by this the type of man who, like Mark, receives a blow, physical or verbal, and whose next reaction—a few beats later—is to understand the reason why the blow was delivered and accept it without response. Such a man, says Bly, is "skipping over the anger entirely." He is not turning the other cheek—he has no cheek to turn.

Appropriate expression (or, for that matter, nonexpression)

of anger is an important skill for anybody to learn, but especially men. That lesson was recently driven home to one of the authors of this book. He was driving a stretch of highway notorious for its speed traps. Sure enough, doing a mile over the limit, he was pulled over (Phase 1: the blow). Because of his work with men's groups he knew it was healthy to acknowledge his feelings: being stopped by a patrolman made him pretty damned mad (Phase 2: anger). To make matters worse, the patrolman's attitude was, shall we say, less than courteous (Phase 2 and a half: more anger). By the time the patrolman tore the ticket off his pad, the driver in question was ready to explode, but he checked himself and said nothing. Instead he proceeded to Phase 3: appropriate response involving assertion, not aggression. He went before the judge and had the pleasure of seeing the reaction on the patrolman's face when the case was thrown out of court and the "offense" was expunged from the driver's record.

Let's look at the stories of Gary and Mark again in this light. Gary experienced a certain frustration: traffic wasn't moving the way he wanted. That can be annoying to anybody. Yet was anger appropriate to the situation, especially to such an intense degree? No. Gary went from Phase 1, "blow," to Phase 2, "anger." But he never moved to the important final phase: understanding and appropriate action. Because Gary was unaware of his feelings and their intensity, he could not choose how to behave. Instead he behaved automatically and destructively.

And what about Mark—discovering his wife and her lover in bed. Does he have a right to feel angry about being betrayed and cheated? You bet he does. But he went from Phase 1 to Phase 3, and never tapped into his inner feeling of anger. His "action" was to withdraw—he went to bed. By ignoring his anger, he skipped an important stage of the process, and thus did nothing helpful to resolve the issue.

Both of these men eventually needed psychotherapeutic help.

Why does one man destroy his car for no good reason, and another man express virtually no emotion when his life has just fallen apart? Helping people sort out such puzzles is where therapists come in.

DIAGNOSIS: ANGER

Many of the men who enter our treatment programs experience problems related to anger. Some of them attempt to "self-medicate" by abusing alcohol or drugs. Some are depressed. Some take out their hostility by beating their wives. Some have medical problems such as ulcers or heart conditions. Some exhibit symptoms of post-traumatic stress. We diagnose these men as accurately as we can to get to the root of the problem and design the most effective treatment.

Our society has not, as yet, recognized anger out of control as a mental disorder in its own right. If you look through the psychiatrist's manual, you won't find "rage" listed as an official diagnosis. You will only see it as a symptom of other conditions.

One of those conditions is called *organic personality syndrome* (was once known as *frontal lobe syndrome*), which is a psychological and behavioral disturbance caused by brain dysfunction that can be temporary or permanent. Temporary problems can stem from alcohol or drug abuse or from infections, metabolic disorders such as diabetes, vitamin deficiencies, or side effects of prescription medications. Usually these problems can be easily identified. If the underlying problem is properly treated, anger or rageful behavior will subside, just as a runny nose will let up when the cold virus has vanished. Permanent brain damage is more serious and can result from injury, tumor, or stroke.

Personality disorders also can lead to problems with rage and violence. *Antisocial personality disorder* is a pattern of thinking and behaving marked by conflict with society, inability to develop strong values and relationships with other people, impulsiveness, and lack of guilt. People with this disorder are often irritable, aggressive, abusive, and promiscuous. Generally, they don't care whom they hurt with their anger and violence.

Borderline personality disorder is a pattern of disrupted relationships leading to intense, misdirected anger, mood swings, feelings of emptiness, inability to tolerate being alone, and actions that cause harm to oneself or others— reckless driving, impulsive fighting. We sometimes see evidence of this disorder in men who threaten to kill themselves or harm their children if their wives leave, for example.

Conduct disorder is a pattern of disobedience or aggressive behavior. People with this condition don't concern themselves too much with the rights of other people or the rules of society. Conduct-disordered individuals get into scrapes with the law, abuse drugs, and experience high rates of physical injuries. They are physically aggressive, cruel, and lacking in guilt or empathy. Typically they come from unstable backgrounds—broken homes, parental problems of abuse, violence, depression, or alcoholism, even abandonment.

Drug or alcohol abuse can provoke angry and rageful behavior. Crack is especially notorious for this side effect. Abuse of steroids, such as by athletes, can lead to a phenomenon users call "'roid rage," marked by explosive outbursts of violence.

The point is that anger is often a symptom—a secondary problem that will abate when the main problem clears up.

It may also be a problem in its own right. In rare cases, we may list a diagnosis that goes by the vague name of *intermittent explosive disorder*. This is the closest thing we have to an "anger disease."

People with this condition are usually males in their teens or twenties. They experience a series of episodes in which they lose control over their aggressive impulses and go on rampages, assaulting people and property. What's striking about these episodes is that the rage is far out of proportion to the insult. It is "the shoelace that snaps" that triggers the violent outburst. These violent spells come on quickly, within minutes, and subside quickly. Afterwards the patient is usually genuinely sorry about what happened, and may reproach himself for his behavior. Between episodes, the impulsivity and aggression subside. Before we diagnose this disorder, we have to rule out all the possible causes of anger, since they are far more likely to be the problem. In fact, this diagnosis is a controversial one; many therapists feel it isn't needed, since almost all of its symptoms are covered in the descriptions of other conditions or disorders.

Recently a condition known as *complex partial seizure disorder*, somewhat like epilepsy, has been found to cause violent outbursts. Brain wave tracings from an electroencephalograph (EEG) can reveal such seizure activity.

One of our patients, a 35-year-old man named Darrell, had been a heavy pot smoker for a long time. Six years ago he quit smoking because he had just gotten married and his wife disapproved. Since then, however, he experienced episodes of rage and violent outbursts with increasing frequency. These episodes erupted at the slightest provocation: a tie-up at a toll booth, a rude remark from a salesclerk. One big problem was that Darrell owned a business making blown-glass figurines for sale to gift shops and boutiques. During his outbursts he sometimes smashed thousands of dollars' worth of stock and once fired an employee who had been with him for years.

When Darrell came in for treatment, his history of marijuana use, and the fact that his outbursts worsened after he stopped, made us suspect that his problem was biological. We took an EEG reading and, sure enough, there was the characteristic pattern of seizures. Darrell responded to an antiseizure medication called Tegretol. He and his wife also needed therapy to help them understand the medical problem, to learn how to reduce the stressors in their lives, and how to handle the problem should it recur.

IMAGES OF ANGER

A man who struggles with anger and rage is at risk. He poses a threat to himself, other people, property, and society as a whole. If he acts out his violence, it is tempting to just throw him into prison and forget him. To do so, however, simply reinforces the social myth that men are disposable. The better approach, not just for the individual person but for our whole culture, is to separate the man's rage from the man. We have to make it clear to him that his violent behavior is illegal, abnormal, even immoral—but to do so without condemning the man himself.

Hard as it may be, we can confront and change unwanted behavior and still honor the man in his struggle.

There's another myth permeating our society today, one we would like to destroy. This myth is spread on countless talk shows, in supermarket tabloids and magazines. It is the myth that says the *only* way to deal with anger is to "let it out." The refrain goes something like this: You're angry at your father, you've been holding it in all your life. If you don't express your feelings, this popular wisdom holds, then you're going to die of a heart attack or some other bolt from the blue.

This myth is dangerous because it is only *half* true. We don't need men who have violent or aggressive thoughts to express them any more than they are already doing. A man who wants to kill someone for changing lanes without signaling, for example, is better off keeping his feelings to himself. What may be "therapeutic" for such men is dangerous to us innocent bystanders.

Sometimes our own field of psychotherapy buys into this myth. Well-meaning but misguided therapists urge all their patients to express their angry feelings. When that happens, the problem can get worse. A violent or angry man may get the wrong message—"It's okay to let out my anger. My therapist said so." In our practice we sometimes refer to this as "gasoline therapy"—it just throws fuel on the fire and makes it burn hotter. We find it better if we apply "water therapy" to cool things down.

Another image therapists often use to describe anger is

the pressure cooker: a man's anger builds and builds. If he doesn't lift the lid and release the pressure, he'll explode. This image, however, is incomplete. We sometimes forget that there's another way to reduce the danger. Instead of lifting the lid, we can *turn off the flame underneath* and let the steam inside cool down. After some time has passed, we can them "lift the lid" without scalding the man, or anyone around him.

How can this be done? One way is to work on changing the thoughts that keep the system heated. We humans often have a kind of "running dialogue" going in our heads, issuing ourselves a series of internal commands. Men who run into a difficult situation might say, "That's it, I can't take it any more," or "I can't stand this," or "No one says that to me and gets away with it." These angry thoughts are like logs thrown onto the fire of anger: they only turn up the pressure. Through therapy people can learn to change those internal commands. Instead of "I can't take any more," for example, a man might learn to tell himself, "This is upsetting me, so I'll walk away."

A patient named Brian told us that when his father got drunk he would get violent. "I was like a fly on the wall," he told us. "I tried to stay out of sight, but if Dad saw me, he'd swat me." In such an environment, Brian learned the wrong message, that hitting was the solution to all his frustrations. When he married, he fell into the same pattern. He tended to draw arbitrary limits—a "line in the sand"—and would warn his wife that if she crossed that line he would hit her. "But sometimes she'd push, and push, and so I'd haul off and smack her. She knew the limits, she had been warned. She knew I only hit her when she deserved it."

In therapy, we worked with Brian to help him realize that *he* was the one who had set those arbitrary "limits" on his wife, and that *he* was the one who could change them. By placing that "line in the sand" a little further away each time, he could reduce—and eventually eliminate—those situations where violence had formerly been a "justified" response. (We also worked with his wife to find out why she tolerated such abuse.)

In our practice, we find it is usually more helpful to *discourage* men with rage or violence problems from expressing their anger. That approach goes against the grain of conventional wisdom, but we have found it a highly effective way of saving the males in our care.

For a moment, think about anger as a kind of habit—an addiction, if you will. Men can reach for their anger the way they reach for the bottle. It becomes their style for dealing with problems and frustrations. Because a display of anger often gets them what they want, they may keep relying on it. In time they become dependent on it. Some people even describe such men as "rage-aholics."

The solution for an alcoholic is to abstain totally. By the same logic, a "rage-aholic" needs to abstain from rage. Of course, many men with this problem aren't thrilled to hear this news, just as a drinker never wants to hear he must give up the bottle. And they've been told by so many sources for so long that expressing anger is the way to release it. What we have found, however, is that expressing anger is self-stimulating. Rage begets rage. Eventually, the violence escalates until it gets out of control. For people like Gary, learning how to abstain removes pressure by turning down the fire.

What about people like Mark, who don't recognize their anger even when it is staring them in the face? They need a different treatment approach. They need to work on discovering their anger. In Bly's term, they need to lose their naïveté about their feelings and get in touch with what's going on inside.

Some people reading this will instantly assume that by urging men to discover their anger, we are opening a Pandora's box. "If a man hasn't found his anger," they will say, "so much the better." Let us be clear. Discovering anger doesn't mean acting on it. When in his therapy Mark finally realized he was indeed furious with his wife, the solution was not for him to go and blacken her eye. But at least he was able to connect with part of himself that he had tried to keep buried. The effort had cost him enormously, draining his energy and leading to physical complaints. Now that his anger was available to him, he was closer to being in touch with the full range of his feelings.

Recently a man came up to us after a talk we gave to the community about men's issues. He said, "I spent fifteen thousand dollars and three years in therapy to discover my anger. I finally found it, and my therapist said I should be very proud. And now you mean to tell me that I shouldn't express that anger?" Not at all, we replied. First, we congratulated him on his discovery. Second, we said, by all means, practice expressing it—as long as you do so in appropriate and constructive ways. In your case, that's good therapy. But there are other folks who don't need any more practice—they are already maestros.

Randy, one of our alcoholic patients with a history of abusive behavior, told us that the previous day his wife had gone to a party without him. She came back raving about having met a semi-famous rock singer who invited her back to his hotel room to listen to tapes of his new songs. Randy said that he had been sober for thirty days, but when he heard that, he really wanted to head for the corner bar. He was furious at her, he said, but managed to contain himself. He told her he was glad she'd had a good time and that she'd had the chance to hear some new music.

We congratulated him heartily on his behavior. "But I lied," he said. "I *was* angry. I thought I was supposed to work on being honest with everybody." In this case, we suggested, it was probably better to lie a little—or at least hold back the full truth. Doing so may have bought him some time to get clear about what was really going on inside. After looking into it further, Randy realized the value of what we were saying. He saw, with surprising insight, that what he *really* felt about his wife's behavior was hurt, fear, and a sense of abandonment. "You tie all those feelings together in a bundle, they kind of look like anger," he said, "but they're really not, are they?"

DISCOVERY

Randy had discovered for himself something that women seem to know instinctively, or have been socialized to view as appropriate: how to sort out and label feelings. Several of the therapists on our staff have noticed that their teenage daughters can say something like, "My best friend made me sad but I was still a little worried that maybe we just misunderstood each other, and I was happy that we were at least still talking. She probably felt like I hated her but I knew deep down she still liked me so we worked it out. I'm glad about that." In contrast, their sons are more likely to say, "I hate Josh. I want to punch his lights out."

Men who suppress their anger are playing on a piano with no black keys; men who know only anger are playing a keyboard with only one note. Our approach is to help men learn the full scale of their emotions, with all its disharmonies.

How can men rediscover and express what their feelings are? One simple way is to teach men the fact that feelings produce bodily sensations, and then train them to recognize what those sensations are. In one exercise, for example, we ask men to think about the saddest thing that ever happened to them, write it down, and then read it aloud to the others in their group. When they finish, we ask them to tell us how their bodies are reacting at that very moment. One man might say, "I feel a kind of tightness around my chest." Another will remark, "There's a stinging feeling in my eyes." We then say, "Okay—*that*'s sadness. Practice saying the words: 'I'm sad.'" Simply by connecting the physical sensations with the name of the emotion, men learn to express their emotions.

Anger sometimes arises from misdirected grief. The man has lost something and doesn't have permission to recognize that loss and mourn it. As an exercise, we ask men to take three pieces of paper and write down the three things that are most valuable in their lives. We tell them to wad up one of those papers and throw it away. They then look at the two remaining ones and think about what they no longer have. This simple but powerful exercise evokes intense sadness. Such raw emotions are like lumps of clay: a man can pick them up, work them, massage them, get to know how they feel, pull them apart, and form them into recognizable shapes.

Another key element in helping men address their anger is to identify the things that trigger rage—and to learn what happens in the moments or days *before* the rage erupts. If we can alert men to realize when the cycle of violence is starting, we can often derail it. An ounce of prevention is worth a pound of fury.

In many cases the trigger for anger is the difference in the ways men and women communicate with each other. Because women are often more verbally oriented than men, they are sometimes able to use language more skillfully and more pointedly. A man may feel that a woman is hammering away at him, pushing him into a corner. He may think she is bringing up old garbage from the past and analyzing facts in seemingly illogical ways. If a woman isn't careful, she may venture into the minefield of personal attack: "You care more about your work than me"; "You're just like your father"; "You're no good." She may even criticize his body or his ability at making love. Whether she is right in her comments is not relevant. The problem is, she may keep attacking without realizing that a man who feels trapped may revert to his primitive instincts—including rage and violence—to free himself. Contrary to the image we have, most men don't want to fight. But they will if they feel cornered.

Rageful men need to understand that they are responsible for their own anger. They need to be shown ways of reacting that defuse anger before it gets out of control. One method is the ancient but effective strategy of counting to ten (or twenty or a hundred or whatever it takes) before saying anything. We sometimes even tell men to take a *physical* step backward before acting. It may also help to take a "time out"—a fixed period in which the man leaves the scene or agrees to say or do nothing for perhaps ten minutes or an hour. If this fails, we advise women to make an escape plan for themselves—plan to spend the night in a motel or with a friend until the situation cools down.

Instead of responding with a statement that begins with "you" ("You always..." or "You never...") we try to teach men to use a different formula called "When you/then I." For example: "*When you* bring up something that happened a year ago, *then I* don't think you're focusing on the immediate problem." "*When you* don't want to have sex with me, *then I* feel unloved." Such an approach avoids personal attacks and helps the man identify what he is feeling.

A therapy group made up of men is one valuable arena for learning these and other strategies. When men take responsibility for supporting other men, powerful things can happen. They share their experiences—their war stories—and discuss what works and what doesn't. We often see an older man "adopt" a younger one, becoming a friend, a peer, a father, and a mentor simultaneously. Such a relationship is empowering for both men, as well as for those who observe it taking shape. Patients like Brian, who hit his wife if she crossed his "line," learn that most other men don't see violence against women as an acceptable option. Such a message coming from other men can often be more powerful than it would coming from a therapist.

In treatment men can discuss and practice alternative behaviors. They can imagine a scene where someone cuts in front them in line at the movie theatre and rehearse their responses. They can learn to ask a waitress to take back a steak that is overcooked or too tough, without having to storm out of the restaurant feeling angry—and still hungry.

Most important, men can learn to be appropriately assertive—not aggressive—within their relationships.

The volcano, the pressure cooker, "rage-aholism"—by whatever name, anger is a threat not just to women and to society but to the man himself. Once we penetrate that shield of anger, however, we find that many men, even the very violent ones, are frightened. They are full of shame, sadness, grief, and fear of losing control. We must not reject these men but must deal with them compassionately. By putting them in touch with their anger we can save these males, and restore to them their sense of control.

Chapter 9

MEN AND WORKAHOLISM, ABUSE, DIVORCE

In the movie *Jaws,* there's a scene where the shark hunter and the scientist get drunk and show each other the scars they've acquired in their lives. They are acting out a basic male ritual: trading war stories, topping each other with yarns of bravery and battles.

Men get many scars in their time, some physical, some emotional. Some scars are a source of pride, earned while defending themselves or standing up for a principle. Other scars, however, are a source of stinging shame, a reminder of endless pain.

RAY

When Ray first entered our men's program, we asked about the obvious mark above his lip, which his moustache only partly covered. "Some guy whacked me with a beer bottle because he didn't like the way I was looking at his girl," he replied. "I paid him back, though. I decked him *and* screwed his woman."

A few weeks later, however, Ray was taking part in a men's group session. Some of the men talked about the times their parents had beaten them or that they had been sexually molested by family members, neighbors, or babysitters. Ray listened thoughtfully; it was obvious the things he heard were affecting him deeply. He then spoke up and recalled how his father used to thrash him and his brother for no reason. "One time Pop was watching television and I asked him a question. He grabbed his beer bottle and smashed me in the mouth. It took twelve stitches to close it up."

A lot of important things happened in that moment.

First, Ray had heard other men revealing their shame and their pain, and he felt empowered to do the same. He realized, too, that he was in a safe place; he could discuss his feelings without fear of being criticized or spurned.

Most significant, he told the truth about his scar for the first time in his life. For years he had suppressed the idea that his father had abused him. The reality was so awful that he had made up stories to disguise it, stories that even Ray came to believe were the truth. Although he spoke aloud to the other men, he was really speaking to himself.

MEN AS VICTIMS OF ABUSE

Physical abuse is just one source of men's scars. More troublesome, in a way, are the scars resulting from verbal, emotional, or sexual abuse. Such scars are invisible. Many men who have them don't even know they're there.

One of the most encouraging developments in the field of psychiatry in the past few years has been society's growing awareness that men suffer a tremendous amount of abuse. "Wait!" some people reading this will think. "Men are the *perpetrators* of abuse, not its victims!"

Let's be clear. We do not deny for one minute that men can be violent, abusive, and cruel. Prisons are overflowing, hospitals and clinics are filled with men who hurt other people.

What we are learning, however, is that in many cases these men are simply repeating the lessons they were taught in the past. A significant percentage of the time, *men who were themselves abused become abusive men.* To blind ourselves to that important fact is to deny the truth, and thus to deny ourselves the chance to remedy the situation. Acknowledging the truth gives us hope of breaking the pattern of abuse, neglect and suffering. Men need to learn to recognize how their emotional and bodily scars came to be inflicted, and how those scars continue to direct their emotions and their actions.

If we can save the males from the damage they endured in the past, we can prevent them from inflicting damage on themselves and on others in the future.

In our men's group sessions, we often discuss sexual abuse, what it is and what it means. Such abuse can take many forms: A 15-year-old girl asking an 8-year-old boy to "play doctor." A babysitter playing "naked games" with her charges. An uncle or cousin or friend or trusted professional asking to touch or be touched.

Once the definition is clear, we then ask participants to close their eyes and indicate if they have ever experienced abuse. Often, over *half* of the men in the room raise their hands. Granted, in our practice we are dealing with men whose problems are severe enough to need professional attention, so the percentage is probably higher than we'd see in the general population. Even so, some nationwide studies estimate that perhaps *one in four men were abused, molested, or neglected as children or adolescents*.

Abuse of men has been called "the last taboo." It doesn't fit our image of men to see them as victims. To admit that vast numbers of young boys have suffered at the hands of their parents or relatives or family friends is to risk exposing the secret shame of millions of people, victims and victimizers alike. To state that men—the aggressors, the violent ones—may have been slapped around or scratched up by their wives or lovers is to turn our image of men inside out. Perhaps if we'd been more open about the problem, we wouldn't be treating such vast numbers of damaged men today.

Let's look at some of the ways abuse occurs, and how its aftershocks can put men at risk.

CHILD ABUSE

A child can be *physically* abused: beaten, neglected, starved. The child can be *emotionally* abused: harsh words, devastating criticism, humiliation, shame. Or a child can be *sexually* abused. If sexual abuse involves a parent or other member of the family, it is called incest, one of society's most explicit taboos.

Our files are filled with terrifying stories of the physical abuse our male patients experienced while young. One man said his parents would drape him from a coat hook on the wall and leave him there for hours if he committed the heinous crime of refusing to eat his eggs. Another had rope burns on his wrists from the times he was tied to his bed at night to keep him from escaping the house. One patient said his parents used his body as their "ashtray," stubbing out their cigarettes on him but always being careful to do so in places that would be covered by his clothing.

Emotional abuse is subtler. A boy whose report card displeases his father may be told he is "a worthless piece of shit" or a "stupid, lazy fuck-up." One patient said his stepfather took exception to the job he did cutting the grass, so he made him do the front yard over again—on his hands and knees with a pair of scissors. Another said that after he fanned out in the ninth inning of a key Little League game, his father refused to speak to him for a week. "I feel that for the last thirty years all I've tried to do is show my father I can be successful, just to make up for that one moment of failure. Only after he died did I realize how futile that goal was, and how I've thrown my life away to prove a meaningless point."

Sexual abuse of children violates all standards of civilization. Even the most hardened criminals reserve their deepest hatred for people who sexually molest children. The most common type of incest involves a man's abuse of his daughter. Abhorrent as such a crime is, the girl may not be the only victim. One patient told us of his worst childhood memory: His father often drove him and his teenage sister to the beach in a van. The father would make the boy stand guard outside while the father had sex with the girl.

It is also a fact that some mothers sexually abuse their sons. It can happen when the mother deliberately fondles the boy's genitals while changing a diaper or giving a bath. It can persist for years as the mother clings to her son to provide emotional (and physical) gratification that her troubled relationship with her husband fails to provide. In one of our men's weekends, a man named Eric revealed that his mother had made him sleep in her bed from the time of her divorce, when he was 2, until he ran away from home at age 15. Boys can experience sexual abuse at the hands of mothers, fathers, older brothers, uncles, family friends.

As a pre-teenager one of our patients, Juan, shared a room with his older brother. At night the brother entered Juan's bed and subjected him to anal intercourse. The next day they both behaved as though nothing had happened. Juan grew up filled with a combination of hate, shame, and guilt, but he kept those feelings locked inside. Even when his brother shot himself to death at the age of 28, Juan felt guilty about being unable to grieve the loss of his brother. Juan entered treatment because of a problem called ejaculatory incompetence: No matter how long he had intercourse he couldn't achieve orgasm and ejaculate. Some men in the group joked that they wished they had his problem. But it was a real concern, because his sexual partners always felt he was withholding something from them and they would eventually leave him, or he would leave them in frustration. In therapy he discovered that, subconsciously, he couldn't bear to do to someone else (a woman) what his brother did to him (ejaculate inside the other person's body).

A boy who has been abused is a future man at risk. Common sense tells us this should be so; only recently, however, have we turned a scientific eye on the problem to confirm in our heads what our hearts have long been telling us. A recent study found that abused children have lower intelligence and are at higher risk of depression, drug problems, and suicide. Previous studies had already found a direct connection between abuse and juvenile arrests and violent crime. Another researcher found that abused children were more likely to get angry, refuse to follow instructions, and to lack enthusiasm. By the time abused children enter school, they tend to be hyperactive, easily distracted, lacking in self-control, and not well liked by their peers. Teachers also tend to give up on such students. Abuse has them on the road to lifelong failure.

Sometimes the abuse is severe enough to drive the child away from the home. At that point they fall into a devastating trap. Left to fend for themselves, they associate with the wrong crowd and end up in the hands of the halfway houses, foster homes, juvenile courts, and, usually, prisons. Once they became old enough to be sentenced to prison, many of the men behind bars have known no other homes than their cells.

All abused children, whether male or female, need saving. Boys, however, are already moving in a society whose socialization puts them at special risk of such problems as anger, substance abuse, and so on. Thus a boy who displays anger or gets into trouble is likely to be dismissed: "Boys are like that, aren't they. What can you do about it?" If the problem is serious, he may be disposed of by getting thrown in jail. Out of society's sight, out of society's mind. We must realize that a child's problems may be just a symptom of deeper trouble: abuse or neglect at home.

As a rule, an abusive man was an abused child. He was brought up believing that he is bad or evil or nasty, because the most important people in his life told him that was the case. During his most vulnerable period of development, he was robbed of self-esteem and denied the chance to have a childhood. He became an adult, but without adult defenses and perceptions. Such men need to learn how their past has shaped their present; they can then learn how to take responsibility for their future. For every male we save today, we save many who may not have even yet been born.

HUSBAND ABUSE

Think about this statistic: Twelve percent of spouses are the targets of violence by their mates. Reading that, you probably automatically assume we're talking about abuse of wives by husbands. And we are. But there's more to the story. The shocking thing is that the same statistic applies in reverse: *Twelve percent of husbands are also violently attacked by their wives.*

The phrase "husband abuse" provokes smirks from some people who can't believe there could ever be such a thing. Warren Farrell notes that centuries ago, in France, men who had been beaten by their wives were held in such contempt that they were made to dress up in women's clothes and were paraded through town riding backward on a donkey. That's a pretty powerful way of socializing men: If your wife slaps you around, you're a contemptible wimp. In this regard, at least, our own society is no more advanced than it was three hundred years ago.

Let us be clear. By discussing abused men, we are by no means attempting to minimize the suffering of women. Wife abuse or beating is a tragic and all-too-common part of our culture. We are simply trying to point out another part of the reality: Men suffer too, and our society is too eager to hold such men up to ridicule, since they go against the cultural stereotype. Rather than tell someone about their shame and endure the twentieth-century equivalent of riding backward on a donkey and in drag, men today prefer to cover up their physical and emotional scars. Society *tells* them that's what they should do. Sooner or later, however, their pain will emerge—as substance abuse, mental illness, or in assaults on people or property. And then society will say, oh, you terrible person, you ought to be locked up.

As is the case with children, abuse of husbands can be physical, emotional, or sexual. Sometimes it is all three, as it was in Adam's case.

Adam is a 45-year-old chemical plant worker. Looking at his six-foot, 240-pound frame, his dark beard, and his snakeskin boots, you wouldn't think he was the kind of guy who would put up with any kind of nonsense. Looking deeper, you'd see a man at risk.

Adam has been married to third wife, Joyce, for eight years. They have two sons, ages 5 and 6. Joyce is "hell on wheels," says Adam. She hates everything he does, from the way he drives to the way he parts his hair. Although she doesn't work outside the home, she expects him to do most of the housework in addition to bringing home the bacon. If he dares oppose her in any way, she gets back at him by hitting him where it hurts: in the bank account. She goes on spending sprees, racking up thousands of dollars in charges. He's tried canceling her cards; she just gets new ones. On the last spree, she bought over ten thousand dollars in furniture—for her *mother's* apartment.

She has other strategies, too. She uses sex as a bargaining chip: If she gets angry, she'll scream, "No sex for a month!" And she means it. Although she is a petite woman, she also attacks him physically—scratching and slapping and throwing things. Adam does nothing to defend himself; he says he was taught that a "hitter" is the lowest form of life. He also thinks she is entitled to hit him; he does have his faults, he says, and she's right to "point them out."

Clearly Joyce has some problems of her own. But she didn't seek help at our clinic; Adam did. It was apparent from the beginning that Adam was in a severely dependent or codependent relationship. He had such low self-esteem that he was virtually unable to defend anything about himself, from his wallet to his right to happiness to his right not to have to duck a punch bowl thrown at him as he walks through his front door. Ironically, he only came to us for psychiatric help because he was scared to do what he really wanted, deep down, to do: get a lawyer and get a divorce. He says he would never have considered getting standard psychiatric treatment, but saw a glimmer of possibility in a program that focused on men's issues.

Of course, it was not the therapist's place to suggest what Adam should do to solve his problem. The goal, as in any psychiatric treatment, was to help him understand his situation and explore the options available for dealing with it. By taking part in a men's group, Adam heard—to his obvious surprise—that he was not the only victim of assault by a wife. His "secret shame" was shared by at least two of the others in the program. He gained perspective on his situation and picked up some practical information on what he might do to correct it. He found the courage to stand up to Joyce, put an end to her physical abuse, and get control of his financial affairs. Most of all he found out about himself—how he contributed to his own victimization, and how he needed to develop a new identity and a healthy self-image.

SEXUAL ABUSE BY OTHER MEN

Recently a young man we'll call Fred was having trouble sticking to his program of abstinence from cocaine abuse.

He was also hurt after the breakup of his relationship with his girlfriend and was thinking about moving to a new part of the country and starting over.

One thing he'd learned in treatment was to talk about his feelings with other people. In the hospital he had made friends with Ernie, another addict in recovery. They had stayed in touch after their discharge. One night Fred called Ernie, who invited him to his house for coffee.

While there Ernie made a sexual move on Fred. Fred ran from the house in terror.

The next night Fred came to his outpatient men's group therapy session and blurted out what had happened to him. He blamed himself; he said "I must have been putting out signals." His biggest concern was, "Am I gay?"

Fred was relieved to hear the other men talk about their own struggles with such issues. Most of them had had similar experiences in their past. They reassured him that he had done nothing to bring on the attack, that he was not at fault. The group talked about how unwanted sexual advances can be just as much a form of abuse for men as they are for women.

According to the Kinsey Institute, at least 25 percent—and probably closer to 33 percent—of all American men have had a sexual experience with another male as teenagers or adults. Studies estimate that homosexuals make up anywhere between 3 percent and 10 percent of the population.

Many men see homosexuality as a direct threat to their masculinity. To defend themselves against such a threat, they take the stance that any affectionate contact between men is disgusting or unnatural. Some men think shouting "Faggot!" is the most harmful insult they can hurl at another man. In extreme cases, men go out of their way to attack gays. Among some groups, "rolling queers" is a Saturday night pastime.

Psychologically, it is sometimes the case that men express antihomosexual feelings because they question their own masculinity. They defend against their fears by going to extremes. They attack a perceived enemy—"queers"—rather than explore their deep feelings toward men.

Fred may not have thought so at the time, but he was very lucky. He had a place to come to—a safe place—where he could bring his problem before a group of men, discuss it openly, and explore his feelings. Our society offers no such "tribal council" to help the members of the tribe deal with issues. In that group, Fred learned that his experience was pretty common—a basically normal part of growing up. Fred said he left the meeting that night feeling "anchored," as he put it. He knew he had done nothing to create the situation. He also said he even found the strength to confront Ernie and tell him that, while he liked him as a person, he wouldn't be coming to him to discuss his problems anymore.

Women can also be sexually abusive to men. One physician we know told us about a subtle form of abuse he encountered shortly after his divorce. Women kept "hitting on him" at parties and social gatherings. At first he enjoyed the attention and the "action," thinking he was making up for the years of sexual frustration with his wife. But soon he began feeling used. He realized the woman weren't really interested in him as a person. They were attracted to him merely because they perceived him as well-off and available. One night two women asked him to join them in a *ménage-a-trois*. While this is a common male sexual fantasy, the physician said his response was not joy, as he might have expected, but fear and even anger. He realized he was being not simply used, but sexually abused by women who saw him as an "easy lay."

OTHER TYPES OF PROBLEMS: WORKAHOLISM

We recently heard a man say, "Any job that permits you to take a vacation is not worth having!" This guy exhibited one of the classic symptoms of workaholism: the inability to stop working without experiencing a new kind of DTs—the "downtime terrors."

The term "workaholic" is more than just a cute term. Work can become an addiction as engrossing as alcohol or cocaine. In a way, it's even worse: Work is a habit that has not just approval from society, but its outright endorsement. After all, work is a "clean" addiction. There's another parallel: Workaholics experience symptoms of withdrawal—feelings of emptiness, uselessness, agitation—when they don't get their "fix" of work.

We've seen how men are socialized to carry out their roles as providers and breadwinners. Obviously, such roles are not just necessary, they can be very positive. Work can be a great way to use one's time, to contribute something valuable to society, to earn rewards, and to build one's sense of self-esteem. One of the contributions of the women's movement has been greater access for women to the jobs and the power of the workplace (although of course there is still much room for growth in that area). What our society has *not* had so far is a counter-movement that encourages men to seek the same kinds of flexibility women continue to claim for themselves: the right to *choose* whether to work outside the home, or inside it. Instead we put men at risk by training them to work—then blaming them for becoming addicted to it.

Our society rewards hard work through money, prestige, power, or fame. Companies look on workers who put in long hours as "devoted" and "loyal." Overachieving results in promotions or perks. Glancing at the pictures of Donald Trump and the bevy of women in his life, it is hard to ignore the message that the Lifestyles of the Rich and Famous includes access to the most beautiful women. The incentives for keeping your nose to the grindstone, in other words, can be pretty high.

Workaholics forget that there is a time to work and a time to rest. They get caught up in the reinforcements their work provides for them. They feel that they can't let up, for fear some great opportunity will pass them by. If they don't grab the brass ring this time around, they'll never get a second chance. Interestingly, studies show that workaholics don't necessarily get more work done than those who work normal hours. They may make hasty or wrong decisions, get bogged down in details, and make other people's jobs harder to carry out.

There are also female workaholics. Some of them are driven by the need to prove themselves to the world, or they feel compelled to seize every opportunity as it whizzes past. Some work extremely hard because they are the only providers for their family. Even so, workaholism is a bigger problem among men because more men work as the sole or primary breadwinners and have been conditioned to elevate self-esteem through work.

Is work a health hazard? Yes indeed. Pressure to perform leads to constant stress, and stress, as we've discussed, causes the body to wear out. Workaholics may drag themselves home exhausted, get too little sleep, and drag themselves out of bed to get cracking early the next morning. They shortchange themselves by not taking advantage of the restorative pleasures life is supposed to offer: family, friends, social and cultural activities. They skip vacations, or, what's almost worse, bring their work along to the shore or the mountain cabin. Often workaholics are susceptible to other addictions: pills or cocaine to get them revved up, alcohol to help them unwind. Workaholics may be trying to work out their own psychological problems, perhaps trying to earn approval from their fathers or to escape an unhappy situation at home. Some work hard to avoid criticism or feelings of failure. Without work, they are self-worthless.

Like their substance-abusing counterparts, workaholics often "hit bottom," in the form of a heart attack or other crisis, before they recognize the problem and their need for help.

People at risk of workaholism need guidance to change their ways. Compulsive work is a habit, and habits can be broken. Educational programs can teach men and their families how to recognize and cope with the problem. Cognitive therapy helps them assess their values and the assumptions they make about their need to work. Behavioral treatment shows them how to learn new ways of acting, such as leaving work at a fixed time each day. Some employee assistance programs address the problem of workaholism. There's even a Twelve Step program called Workaholics Anonymous. Of course, talking about the problem within a group of men can also make a difference. A man can certainly "sponsor" a fellow overworker on his road to recovery.

DIVORCE

Today the odds are about even that a marriage will end in divorce. The stereotype of women is that they are more dependent on relationships for their sense of self-worth. The truth is that in terms of emotional cost, marriage is harder on women, while divorce is harder on men.

Studies consistently find that women are more frustrated and dissatisfied by their marriages than men. More wives than husbands consider their marriage unhappy, more regret their marriage, and more seek divorce than men. Perhaps women are socialized to expect more out of being married, while men, in typical stoic fashion, may feel, "Hey, things could be worse."

Divorce is a serious risk for men. A nationwide study found widowers suffer mental illness, commit suicide, contract diseases, and die in accidents at a much greater rate than widows. Married men live longer than single men, even though they experience a higher number of stressors, such as parenthood and pressure to provide for a family, which usually don't crop up outside of marriage. The message is clear: to live long and prosper, men should get married, stay married, and remarry if necessary.

Divorce drastically changes the roles a man plays. Obviously the day-to-day routine of being a husband goes out the window. But in many cases he loses his role as father as well. A divorced woman may become a single mother, but a divorced man typically becomes just single. One of our patients, an airline baggage handler, told us he doesn't visit his kids anymore. "I tried a bunch of times, but my ex-wife gave me a lot of hassle about the arrangements. Then I got laid off when the airline folded, so I couldn't pay child support. My wife said, 'No cash, no kids.' After a while she turned them against me so much they even stopped calling me, so I just gave up." On further investigation, we found out this man had been a good father and had tried to continue in that role, but he felt so inadequate and hopeless that he quit trying. Our treatment focused especially on saving this male in his role as father.

Divorce puts kids at risk, too. In *Iron John,* Robert Bly writes: "When women, even women with the best intentions, bring up a boy alone, he may in some way have no male face, or he may have no face at all." If the son is deprived of access to his father, and is given no positive male role model, he may be looking for Father the rest of his life.

The stereotype of the "wicked stepmother" crops up often in fairy tales. Psychologically speaking, it's easier to accept evil in a stepmother than in the child's natural mother. But as is often the case with fairy tales, there is a deeper truth at work. When a parent remarries, it can be difficult, if not impossible, for the new spouse and the children to form a bond. It can take an average of two years for children to adjust to the new situation—and many remarriages only last about twice that long. Children may feel the new man in the house is an intruder, someone who wants to come between them and their mother. He becomes the "wicked stepfather," even if he is trying to be the best father he knows how. If he has children of his own, he may have to act as disciplinarian and mediator, opening himself up to charges of favoritism toward his kids and bias against hers.

Another danger is that a new stepfather may feel he has to constantly prove himself. The woman may have married him not just because she loves him but because he would make a good "role model" for her kids. Thus he takes on a role, not just as husband and stepdad, but as "Grand Exalted Symbol of All Things Masculine and a Counterexample to that No-Good Bastard, Your Ex-Father." Pretty tough assignment. Often a newly blended family falls back into the same emotional and behavioral patterns they followed before the divorce, which only adds to the problem.

Men need help, not just during and after their divorce

but when they remarry. Making time to be with other men, whether in a support group or a less formal arrangement, is not a luxury, not just "time away from the ball and chain." It is necessary for a man to develop a positive sense of himself, to regroup, reassess, and restore his strength before shouldering the burden of his roles again.

EATING DISORDERS

The vast majority of people with eating disorders are women. It is a mistake to conclude, however, that these problems don't affect men. They do, and they can be just as deadly. Apart from the serious physical consequences of eating disorders, psychological factors play an important role. As a rule, the presence of an eating disorder often suggests that a person is trying to use food as a substitute for confronting and dealing with feelings of powerlessness.

There are three main types of eating disorders: obesity, bulimia, and anorexia. All of these pose serious threats to physical and psychological health; in some cases, especially in anorexia, the person may die.

Obesity is a problem of overweight that threatens the person's mental and physical health. One of our patients was referred to us from a nearby diet clinic. Solomon had ballooned up to 300 pounds and was getting nowhere with his program. He is the gentlest, friendliest, most easy-going guy you'd ever want to meet. It turns out, however, that Solomon had never allowed himself to feel, let alone express, anger. As a child he had coped with upsetting feelings by eating. In treatment he realized that, as an adult, he was still "stuffing down" his feelings by burying them in an avalanche of food. By confronting his anger, he gained a lot of control over his appetite.

Bulimia is a pattern in which people go on binges and then take action to rid themselves of their meal. Typically a bulimic induces vomiting, but others rely on laxative abuse, excessive exercise, or some combination of these strategies. Matt, age 24, was a bulimic. While in treatment for depression, he revealed that he often ate huge amounts of food in one sitting. "It's no problem," he said, "because I burn it off during exercise." Indeed, Matt often worked out twice a day, for a total of nearly twenty hours a week. Matt's whole focus was his body. He was good-looking with a fine physique, but he had serious trouble forming and keeping relationships with women. We soon realized that Matt built his entire sense of self-worth on the external aspects of his appearance. He wanted to achieve the "perfect male form." Concentrating on his pecs and delts, however, meant he never had to confront the emptiness he felt inside. Part of Matt's treatment involved teaching him about the havoc his eating pattern wreaked on that body he prized so highly. Matt said he binged because he needed the energy for exercise. In therapy, however, he learned that the reverse was true; he exercised as an excuse to binge. When that discovery hit home, he realized he could break the pattern—he could stop exercising excessively, and thus not need to eat so much, and still keep his physique.

Anorexia occurs when people deliberately starve themselves, eating minuscule quantities or nothing at all in a desperate effort to be thin. A patient named Gabe was admitted because his weight had dropped nearly 20 percent over a few months. In therapy we learned that Gabe had some serious problems at home. At 22 years old, he lived with his parents, who insisted on doing everything for him. They told him what to wear, what to do, what friends he should and should not have. Let him show interest in a girl, and that was the end of the relationship, since "no one was good enough" for their little boy. They wouldn't let him get a job, and supplied him with all the spending money he wanted. The problem reached a crisis when Gabe said he wanted to study to be a veterinarian at a school in another state. His parents undermined all his efforts to apply to the school. Eventually Gabe started starving himself. Put simply, Gabe was unconsciously trying to control the one aspect of his life left to him: what went into his body. By refusing to eat he was showing who was the ultimate boss over his fate. When he achieved that breakthrough, he saw that he could reach the same goal through other means. His treatment focused on his need to establish his own sense of personal autonomy and self-worth, to extricate himself from the family bonds, and to create a life of his own—apart from his identity as a starving man.

LEARNING DISABILITIES

As we discussed in Chapter 4, men are genetically more vulnerable to certain learning disorders than women. The problems these disorders cause can be troublesome. Our society is devoted to success, but a learning disability can make it difficult for a child to succeed in school. Early problems in this regard can set him on the "failure track." Although bright, he may be put into a class of slower students. He may not have access to the best resources or the most perceptive teachers. Because no one expects much of him, he will not try very hard. In our society, a man who is labeled a failure, especially if his "failure" occurs early on in life, will be treated as a highly disposable individual.

A boy who has trouble learning may be seen as "unmotivated" or assumed to have a low IQ. Boys will be boys, the educator may think. He'd rather be out playing baseball than conjugating verbs. Such labels mean that an underlying problem such as dyslexia or attention deficit-hyperactivity disorder (ADHD) may go unrecognized. The child may be trying, but may get extremely frustrated that he can't make sense of the words on the page or follow a series of instructions in the proper order. If he tries and fails, he may be ridiculed. If he misspeaks in front of the class or turns in an unacceptable project, the other students might laugh at him or cause him to feel ashamed. He will naturally think, If I can't do this, I might as well not even try. The downward spiral begins: I'm a failure, I give up, why bother. Such children often drop out or hang around with the wrong crowd. If he starts using pot or drinking alcohol before, during, or after school, he's in double jeopardy. The chemicals in his brain, even a week after drug or alcohol use, make it harder for him to concentrate on, learn, and retain new information. Also, the younger his age when he starts drinking or drugging, the greater the likelihood he'll become an alcoholic or an addict.

Learning disabilities can be detected early by trained professionals. Once identified, they can be dealt with through special educational programs. A boy at risk may become a man at risk; breaking the cycle early is an important way of saving the males.

As we've seen in this section, men earn their scars in many ways. Let's turn away now from the sources of pain and consider the ways we can help ease the pain.

Part III

SAVING THE MALES

Prologue

Echoes from the Talking Stick

The stick is passed... the healing continues....

Seth, 44, a welder: "I thought my divorce would get rid of most of my problems. It didn't. I was alone more, I drank more, I lost touch with a lot of friends. Some days I could barely make myself get up in the morning. People told me to 'snap out of it' and 'get a grip.' I wasn't even sure what it was I was supposed to get a grip on. How can you ask for help when you don't even know what the problem is?"

Derek, 31, a buyer for a men's clothing chain: "I was brought up believing guys never let on when something was bothering them. You had trouble, you dealt with it. You clean up your own mess. Anybody who can't handle things on his own—he's not a man, he's a failure. As I get older, though, it seems like trying to fix your problems without help is like do-it-yourself brain surgery. Society just doesn't make it very easy on a guy who knows he's in trouble and wants to get out of it."

Kirk, 57, a fundraiser: "As a kid I remember running to my mother when I got hurt or mad. When I was about ten or so, some friends gave me a lot of shit about that—'Momma's boy,' 'candy-ass,' that sort of thing. I wanted to show them I was one of the gang, so I made a big deal out of turning my back on my mother, and I think I really hurt her. A couple of times I went to my dad to tell him something important. He didn't want to hear it. 'That's your mother's department,' he'd say, or 'Don't bother me with that nonsense.' I cut myself off from my mother, and then found out my father wasn't there when I needed him. I've never forgiven him."

Greg, 29, an aerospace engineer: "I tried to get help, to make myself a better person and learn how to form better relationships. I went to some therapy groups. I tell you, though, I had to listen to a lot of people say a lot of really terrible things about men. Not just the group members—

some of the group leaders, too. To listen to them, you'd think men were nothing but a bunch of liars and cheaters and rapists and all of them should be thrown into jail. I wanted to work on my problems, not to be targeted as *the* problem just because I was a guy. One night I walked out and never went back."

Curtis, 40, a pilot: "I think men need to teach each other how to be men."

Chapter 10

Men Misunderstood, Misdiagnosed, Mistreated

One of the battles in the war between the sexes has been fought in the field of psychiatry. The skirmish can be traced to the time when Sigmund Freud confessed, "Despite my thirty years of research into the feminine soul, I have not yet been able to answer...the great question that has never been answered: What does a woman want?"

Some members of the women's movement claim that psychiatry is dominated by the heirs of Freud, men who, like their mentor, haven't a clue about women's needs. They claim that men based the principles of psychiatry on their own craziness, projecting their own gender biases onto their female patients. Certainly, everyone in the helping professions—medicine, psychology, social work—must be on guard against such bias.

To claim that psychiatry is biased against women, however, is to perpetuate a dangerous myth. The fact is, *psychiatry has been much more successful at helping women than men*. While many of the leaders in psychiatry, psychology, and social work have been men, most of the people doing therapy with patients are women. Most therapeutic techniques are based on what can be called the "female model." That is, treatment is designed to reveal and explore feelings, to develop better methods of communication, and to improve relationships among people.

Feelings, communication, relationships—valuable for any human being, but especially prized by women. To accuse the entire field of therapy of ignoring women's needs is to ignore the reality: If anything, treatment has catered to women, *sometimes at the expense of men*.

Consider this: Of every ten patients who walk through the door of a clinic, between six and nine of them will be women. Naturally, psychiatry has had to serve the needs of those who come in for treatment. Another point: Much of the social debate about gender roles has actually been debate about *women's* roles. That was necessary, and continues to be so. In the process, however, the need for understanding about men's roles and the changes they must make was shoved to the bottom of the social agenda. As a result, the helping professions have lost sight of men's special needs. If the situation continues, society will pay the price: ever-increasing rates of male depression, substance abuse, violence, and suicide.

FACTS AND FEELINGS

A too-typical scenario: A guy—let's call him Barry—finally decides he needs help. He's not cutting it at work; his wife is complaining that he is being withdrawn and silent; nothing makes him happy, nothing rings his bell. Compared to the other guys he knows, he feels like a loser. He is, as we sometimes say, in a one-down position.

He goes to a counselor. At some point during their conversation the therapist, who has been doing this routine so long that it is almost automatic, says, "Barry, I hear you telling me the *facts* of the situation, but you're not telling me your *feelings*. I can't work with you if you don't talk about what's going on inside you." Barry tries, but because he is a Typical Male in our twentieth-century culture, he has a tough time even identifying what his feelings are.

Some time passes. Again the therapist says, "Barry, you're blocking yourself. Don't tell me your thoughts. Tell me how you feel." By this point Barry is starting to sweat. He's talking, but he's not being heard. However well-meaning the therapist's intentions, however sweetly phrased the words, Barry is picking up an underlying message: "Not only are you a wimp for having a problem so serious that you need help, you are a failure at the therapy game—you can't show your feelings." Now Barry is in a "two-down" position. He has two strikes against him.

There aren't many men who are willing to stick around for strike three. And who could blame them?

It's pointless to expect a person who doesn't know Japanese to understand a conversation in that language. Similarly, it's a waste of time to expect a man who was not trained, as most women are, in the language of feelings to understand a conversation using the vocabulary of emotions. We don't tell a man he should feel ashamed because he can't speak

Japanese. Why should we shame him for being emotionally deprived—*as society raised him to be?*

If men are to benefit from treatment, therapists have to understand and address their needs. Getting in touch with feelings and expressing them appropriately must become the goal of the process, not its method.

WHY GENDER-ORIENTED TREATMENT *IS* VALUABLE

Here's a little parable: If at a distance we see a person standing on a street corner, dressed strangely, waving wildly, and babbling incoherently, we might conclude the person is crazy and we steer clear of him. However, if we realize that we are in Des Moines, Iowa, the person is a Russian tourist, and a cab has just driven off with his suitcase, the problem—and some approaches to its solution—becomes clear. Similarly, if we look at a man at risk and account for all the facts of his situation—his maleness being one of the most important of those facts—then we are well on the way toward offering him the kind of help he needs.

Achieving a fundamental change in a person's way of thinking and behaving can be difficult. By bringing men together in groups independently of women, we reduce by one the factors that can disrupt the process of healing.

Women are the experts when it comes to feelings, and feelings are the key to treatment. When men meet in groups with women, they sense that they may be out of their league in terms of emotional understanding. Again, they may feel "one-down." It often happens that a man who tries to express his feelings in a mixed group is criticized or ridiculed: "How can you say that?" "What a chauvinistic idea!" "Typical male thinking!" One remark like that, and he may clam up forever.

Sometimes, too, men may be embarrassed by their feelings. For example, some of our patients, like Allan whom we met earlier, have survived devastating accidents at petroleum or chemical plants. When women are in the room, men want to project an image of control. They are less willing to talk about how scared they were. To do so means they might appear weak or unworthy of respect—not "macho." Without women present, however, a man is more willing to share what is really going on inside. He knows the other men are also struggling with the same problems. If he's wrong, the others will tell him so, but usually in language he can understand and that doesn't rob him of his confidence in his maleness.

Some women blame men for all of their problems, and in some cases they have good cause for complaint. Often, however, men participating in a mixed group feel exposed and vulnerable, as if they have been personally designated as the targets for all of the women's pent-up hostility and rage. Thus what may be therapeutic for the women may be devastating for the men. In all-male groups, male-bashing simply isn't an issue. Instead we can focus on other problems: social roles, stereotypes, the need for better relationships. That isn't to say men may not vent their gripes about women; they most certainly will, if that's what is needed. Hopefully, though, they do so in a constructive way by learning what responsibility they share in creating the problem—and in learning the techniques needed to resolve it.

Men and women communicate in different ways. Men-only groups allow members to talk with less risk that something will get lost in the translation. In a men's group, a participant may talk about his marriage, saying, "I come home every night, I always hand over my paycheck, I'm good to the kids, I don't gamble or have affairs—why is my wife so angry just because I don't say 'I love you' enough?" The other men will understand instinctively that this man demonstrates his love for his wife through actions, not words. In a mixed group, however, the women are likely to correct him: "Yes, but you're not *saying* it!" The women may criticize him; the men will teach him.

It's a fact of life: Men need the chance to be with other men. For some time now, women have demanded their right to enter all-male bastions: clubs, bars, locker rooms, Princeton dining halls. True, when such clubs are formed merely to exclude women from making business contacts or to deny them other rights, then they are harmful. It's ironic, however, that some women deride men's ability to form close bonds with each other, and then deny their right to gather among themselves in situations where those bonds might be formed. Men's therapy and support groups are healthy alternatives. They provide opportunities for men that may be missing in their relationships at work, among their friends, or in their leisure activities.

WHY MEN RESIST TREATMENT

As David Letterman might say, here are the Top Ten reasons men resist getting the treatment they need.

- *Denial:* Refusing to admit there's a problem in the first

place. Alcoholics and substance abusers especially are masters at rejecting the idea that anything is wrong.
- *Disruption:* Treatment can interfere with the daily business of living. Not all companies will grant men the time off from work that would be needed to get better; if they enter the hospital they may get cured—but they may be out of a job. A related problem is that they may not have medical plans that cover their expenses, and so they refuse to get help. If they do get treatment but it doesn't offer all the services they need, they are at risk of relapse.
- *Self-image:* For men, asking for help is a sign of weakness. Society teaches men to value strength, independence, self-reliance. To suggest that a man needs help triggers a primal fear within him, a fear that he may be inadequate.
- *Embarrassment:* Too often our society stigmatizes people with psychiatric problems. Once a person is labeled as a loser, that label tends to stay with him for the rest of his life. What we need is a society that cheers the man who takes steps to correct his problem, rather than making him feel like a fool for admitting his problem in the first place.
- *Low self-worth:* Men learn that they are disposable, that they are insensitive losers, that they have little value beyond their ability to support a family. Why bother fixing up a rusty car that's missing a few key parts? Might as well just throw it away....
- *Fear of dependence on others:* Men are taught to take control of their lives. To reverse that lesson and turn themselves over to another's care—to become "one-down" voluntarily—is extremely difficult for most men.
- *Fear of openness:* Men aren't trained to discuss their problems with other people. It just isn't a habit for them to complain or reveal that they are suffering. They can't imagine joining a support group and talking about their lives to a roomful of strangers.
- *Fear of blame:* Most of the time, a woman brings the man into treatment or pressures him to "fix himself." *He's* to blame for the problem, not her. Men naturally resist going for help if they suspect they will be held personally accountable for all the sins men have committed against women since light first dawned. They must feel they will be safe from blame and will be heard if they are going to take the risk of exposing their vulnerable side.
- *Lack of available treatment:* Many parts of the country

may have no treatment programs available that can address the needs of a man at risk. Many outpatient groups meet at night, but a man who works the late shift or who has to hold down two jobs may not be able to attend. Sometimes men simply don't get the word about programs that are open to them. Gender-specific treatment is a new idea, but it's catching on.
- *Things haven't reached the "crisis" stage:* Men seldom come in for treatment until some disaster knocks their lives totally out of control. A drug user faces a court trial; an alcoholic is threatened with loss of his job or family; a rageful man is seen as a menace to society. We need to find ways to overcome men's resistance to reassure them that help is available, that they can get such help before they hit bottom, and that they will be safe during the process.

WHY MEN DON'T STAY IN TREATMENT

Getting men into therapy is one problem. *Keeping* them there is another.

For one thing, overcoming problems that are related to gender doesn't happen overnight. It takes years for society to mold a man; it can take years to undo the damage. The stereotypical male is impatient—he may want instant success, or a magic pill that will cure him of his PTSD or his anger. If he can't see results, and fast, he is very likely to walk out the door.

Of course, the benefits of treatment can be hard to spot, at first. A man's marriage may be in trouble because he doesn't talk to his wife. After treatment, it may take months for him to put what he has learned into practice. Similarly, if he erupts in rage when challenged by people in authority, he will need exposure to a number of such situations before he can be sure he has mastered the self-control strategies he learned during treatment. Therapy takes place in a controlled environment; the actual cure comes over time, out in the "real world."

Some men leave treatment because the therapists don't speak his language. Women often complain about male therapists, saying they just don't understand what it's like to be a woman. Men are fair in making the same complaint about some women therapists, who may not fully realize what it's like to be a man. In order to reach men, therapists must know how to "talk male talk." They must recognize that when a man says what he thinks, he indirectly reveals what he feels. If he finally opens up but suspects that he is not being heard, or not being understood, he may leave—and he would be right to do so.

Some men drop out of outpatient treatment because it does not fit their schedules. They may work odd hours or have family responsibilities that prevent them from participating. Men's programs must take such needs into account or they are not serving their patients.

For many men, standard psychotherapy is too passive. "Sitting in a room emoting for hours is not what guys do best," one patient remarked. "Too much talk, not enough action," another said as he resigned from a group. A program that is gender-oriented will recognize the value of teaching men about themselves through active methods. As we'll see in the next chapters, some of these methods include experiential therapies, such as obstacle courses, and psychodrama groups, where problems are acted out.

Too often treatment programs regard patients as generic warm bodies. Therapists proceed as if a man's gender meant nothing in terms of his upbringing, his dealings with society, his perceptions of the world, the roles he plays. To make ourselves gender-blind means we may be unable to see a solution to the problem.

Finally, men may not stay in treatment if it fails to connect them to the world of other men. By bringing men together to discuss their wounds and their worries, they draw on each other's strengths and help overcome each other's sense of weakness.

CHANGE IN THE AIR

Robert Bly stresses that men's therapy must go beyond words and tap into other kinds of healing energy, such as that stored in the forces of nature. In characteristically whimsical style, he says therapists will show they understand this principle "when they insist on doing therapy with a cow in the room."

There are many encouraging signs that the "cow"—that is, treatment for men that goes beyond the standard approaches—is being made a part of more and more programs for men around the country. During the last decade or so society has taken steps to recognize and honor men's special needs. Recently some researchers identified the main health care needs of men today:

- Open talk about health concerns
- Consideration of the male role

- Understanding the physical and mental health risks specific to men
- Discussion of how lifestyle—occupation, leisure, personal and sexual relationships—can contribute to risk
- Exploring sex roles during times of rapid social change
- A flexible and accessible health-care system responsive to men, their occupations, the special needs of fathers, older men, and so on

Many social forces are at work to bring about these changes in the approach to men's treatment. The women's movement made us aware that a gender-specific approach can be of great value. Employee assistance programs are finding that programs focused on men's needs can be more effective and efficient. Insurance companies, concerned about costs, are also seeing the wisdom of programs that address gender-related issues. Media coverage of men's issues is helping spread the word (as well as some confusion) about the trend.

One key change in society's approach to men's treatment has been the growing awareness that men continue to develop in stages over their lifetimes. As Robert Bly puts it, "By the time a man is thirty-five he knows that the images of the right man, the tough man, the true man which he received in high school do not work in life. Such a man is open to new visions of what a man could be."

It's become a cliché to speak of men who are suffering through a "midlife crisis." Yet to ignore such crises, to discount their impact and their importance, is to mistreat men. Men may need guidance, first to help them learn that such changes are happening, then to help them get the most out of the transition. A man in this stage wants the second act of his life to play differently from the first. As Daniel J. Levinson points out in his book *The Seasons of a Man's Life*, "A special task of middle adulthood is to become more aware of both the child and the elder in oneself and others." Ideally, at midlife, a man reunites with those parts of himself that he may have ignored or suppressed. The goal of gender-specific treatment for men is to bring about that reunion and, once it has occurred, to provide good answers to the question, "What now?"

Another important change in treatment is the awareness that many of the symptoms men experience are directly related to their roles in life. By lifting the burdens of their restrictive roles, we can remove some of the pressures that contribute to their problems.

We are also beginning to recognize that men today lack any kind of meaningful rite of passage into manhood. In primitive cultures, boys are taken by the elders and shown, clearly and dramatically, what is expected of them as adult members of the group. Our melting-pot society, however, has no single, definitive initiation rite that tells all its males they have passed a milestone in their lives. By no means can a treatment program for men serve as any kind of substitute for a true rite of passage. *But it can help.* Such a program can teach men what it means to be a mature modern male. It can also show them how to work toward achieving maturity in ways they may have neglected during other stages of their development.

Programs can also go far in solving another key problem: men's isolation—from society, from family, from themselves. By teaching men to be so fiercely independent and self-sufficient, society has robbed men of the chance to develop strong, life-sustaining connections. In contrast, teaching them the value of connectedness can reduce their level of aggression, frustration, and fear. At the most basic level, helping men end their isolation from the emotional and physical signals coming from their bodies will put them at lower risk from the hazards of stress and physical illness. Reducing isolation empowers men to draw strength from their relationships with wives, children, even other men, and show them how to share their own strengths as lovers, husbands, friends, and mentors.

MEN TREATING MEN

There's an old saying: Give a man a fish, and for a day he will not go hungry. But teach a man how to fish, and he will never go hungry again.

Those best qualified to teach a man how to *be* a man—not just for a day, but for always—are other men. A male-oriented approach helps men understand the impact their gender has on their lives: socially, politically, economically, physically, emotionally. Only a man can understand the guilt and suffering of another man, and show him how to get free of such a deadly burden. It takes a man to recognize another's struggle, to validate his efforts, and to honor his worth.

Our programs at the Wetcher Clinic and at Baywood Hospital were among the first to create an alternative approach to psychiatric therapy for men, programs which consider men's situations from a gender-specific point of view. We'll describe our approach in detail in the following chapters. We believe such programs go a long way in addressing the men's health care agenda outlined above. Offering a treatment plan for men *as* men means they will no longer be misunderstood, misdiagnosed, and mistreated.

When men treat men, the healing may be forever.

Chapter 11

A New Approach

Men are discovering that, through the forces of socialization, some of their masculinity has been torn out by its roots. In the process they have suffered deep wounds.

Healing wounds is the work of medicine. Yet medicine and the other helping professions have been slow to see that, like age or social background, maleness is a factor we must take into account in diagnosing a man's problems and finding a remedy.

This chapter describes the approach to healing we find valuable as psychiatrists and psychotherapists. There are other ways to achieve the same goals. But over the past several years we have treated hundreds of troubled men. We know first-hand these methods work.

THE MEN'S FORUM

Our program, known as the Men's Forum, tackles problems from the men's perspective. There are two branches: the inpatient program, offered through Baywood Hospital, and the outpatient program, offered at the Wetcher Clinic, both in Houston, Texas. The authors of this book, working with others on the clinic staff, designed, implemented, and now run the programs.

Our interest in helping men is more than just professional. We, too, have wrestled with issues directly related to our own male roles. We have seen, for example, that achieving intimacy with our sons is a totally different experience than with our daughters. We have struggled to form loving relationships with our wives, our parents, our friends. During our earlier careers in business or the military, we felt the pressure to sacrifice ourselves for the good of our families or our country. Now, as healers, it is our goal—it is our duty—to share our understanding with other men.

Thus we created an all-male unit at Baywood Hospital. At a given time there are perhaps twenty-four men in the hospital unit, whose diagnoses range from depression to substance abuse. The care they receive includes many of the same basic elements as would be found in any modern psychiatric facility. Such care is based on what we call the medical model, because it regards the patient's condition as a disorder requiring a combination of talk therapy, stress reduction techniques, active therapies, and, if appropriate, medication. The main difference is that these patients take part in group therapy sessions for men only so they can focus on issues related to gender. By living together during their stay in the hospital (typically four weeks), these men form strong and healthy bonds with each other. We often sense that as much healing takes place around the men's unit pool table as in any of our structured sessions.

The Men's Forum at the clinic is an outpatient program that offers services that vary according to each person's needs. There are support groups, individual and group therapy sessions, and counseling for couples and families. Treatment takes into account the broad context of the men's lives: work, personal and family relationships, problems with self-esteem, and difficulties adapting to society's ever-changing expectations. Each month perhaps fifty men are taking part in Men's Forum activities at the clinic. Some are there to work on specific problems; others are there because they want to grow as human beings.

One key element is the Emerging Male Weekend, during which men gather to learn and share through rituals, talk sessions, body movement, workshops, and problem-solving activities. Some of those who participate are currently active in, or are graduates from, the Men's Forum programs. Patients staying at Baywood Hospital sometimes take part. Others, ranging from businessmen to clergymen, come simply because they have heard about the weekends and wish to join in a community of men. We've sprinkled scenes from a typical weekend throughout this book and will say more about the topic in the next chapter.

These programs have been successful enough to allow us to expand our reach. For example, we sponsor a program called Men Treating Men, in which other therapists meet to share information about helping their male patients. We also give public talks, conduct workshops, and write articles for local publications.

In all our programs, the unifying theme is that men today need to be honored for who they are and what they have experienced. We believe there is value in male energy.

Men need approval from other men, and must have a safe place where they can express what they feel without shame, without blame. The ultimate goal of any psychotherapy is to give people greater freedom of choice in their thoughts, feelings, and actions. The participants in our program learn this means freedom from having to live their lives according to someone else's stereotyped idea of what maleness is all about.

GETTING THROUGH: THERAPEUTIC STRATEGIES

Men today often have trouble expressing what it is they feel. Through therapy, they can learn. We call this learning the *psychoeducational* method.

We begin by asking, how can we teach this man about himself? One way is to identify the various roles he plays in life. Some of these roles are obvious: son, husband, father, employee. Some may not be so obvious: brother, uncle, friend, mentor. We then identify which of those roles may be giving him grief. Perhaps his marriage is falling apart. Maybe it's a conflict with his parents. Sometimes he is having trouble holding a job—what is it about his role as worker that is rubbing him the wrong way?

Each role comes with its own "script." The trouble is, sometimes society forgets to give men a copy of that script to let them know what is expected of them. In therapy we discuss what society demands from men—and what happens when they fail to live up to those demands. Sometimes the role he plays is not appropriate for the situation; perhaps he acts like the "boss" with his wife and kids or acts like a "husband" with his secretary.

Next—and this is crucial—we point out that each role triggers a different set of feelings. As a father, a man whose 15-year-old son stays out till three in the morning may feel a complex blend of worry, anger, fear—perhaps even jealousy. As a worker, this same man, racing to meet a deadline, may feel frustration or excitement. For many men, treatment is the first chance they've ever had to consider what feelings are, and to realize that feelings can change as circumstances change. The Eskimos have many words to describe "snow." Similarly, men need to learn a broader vocabulary to describe their feelings and to recognize the distinctions between, for example, anger and frustration and sadness.

Psychoeducation does not mean we teach men *how* to feel. It means we help them identify *what* they are feeling.

We then discuss the options they have for responding to those feelings.

Educating men about their roles and feelings takes time. We can't undo a lifetime of damage in four weeks or four months. At best we can start the process and show them how to keep the process going after they leave treatment.

A man's best teacher is another man. Today men no longer have access to a "council of elders" who can offer perspective and advice. In groups we try to make men aware that those who have "been there" are the best ones to turn to. An elder can be simply the oldest one in the group. However, a young man who has completed several weeks of therapy can be an "elder" to someone just entering the program. We encourage men to stay in touch with each other after leaving the program, to keep building on what they have learned.

Another key method is to help men see how they get into trouble because of the ways they've been taught to think. Through a method known as *cognitive therapy*, we look at—and change—negative beliefs, attitudes, and perceptions.

For example, society teaches men to believe "I have to be strong, in control, logical. I can't be weak; I must do battle against my competitors; I must always win." Another belief is, "My manhood is defined by my status in life—my work, my income." Many times such beliefs take the form of a "should" statement: "I *should* not show my feelings"; "I *should* always be the breadwinner." Men have labored under these beliefs for so long that they never stop to question them. They just obey them, as an actor obeys his script.

Cognitive therapy makes a man aware of his underlying beliefs, perhaps for the first time. More important, therapy then "reprograms" beliefs, replacing those that are negative or false with those that are positive and true.

A man might find, for example, that his fundamental belief is "I should always compete with other men." If he realizes that such an attitude makes it difficult for him to be friends with anyone, he can learn to replace that belief with a newer, more flexible one: "I can cooperate with men to achieve my goals."

One way to drive the point home is for the man to picture himself acting according to his new belief. Through this method, known as visualization, he forms an image of what he wants to do and rehearses the scene in his mind. When he faces the situation in real life, he is prepared. Like an actor, he knows his lines—and they are ones he wrote for himself.

Through *behavioral therapy* men learn new ways of acting by trying out behaviors and getting some feedback. For example, one of our patients, who prided himself on his appearance, said he got furious whenever anyone criticized his taste in clothes. In his men's group, he practiced new ways of responding to criticism: ignoring the other person, laughing it off, asking for more information, even agreeing to change his outfit. He saw that some alternatives might work for him, but some would not. In any case, he now had a wider repertoire of responses than he had before. And he had practiced those alternatives in a safe place—the therapy group—and learned from other men as he went along.

Another important component of our program is *experiential therapy*, which involves building trust and a sense of teamwork through challenging experiences. We give the men an objective, such as "build a rope bridge and get all of your men from Point A to Point B without touching the ground." The purpose is not to build the bridge, but to learn how to work together to solve a common problem. In the process men must think, prepare, plan, trust, communicate, and cooperate—skills that are vital back in the "real world." After each experience, the men talk about what happened, how things might have gone differently, and how they felt during the event. In addition to being challenging and fun, experiential therapy works for men because it is *active*.

TYPES OF GROUPS

Group sessions are the backbone of the Men's Forum. In a group, men can exchange their feelings and get feedback. The greatest learning—and the greatest healing—takes place, not doctor to patient, but man to man.

We create a number of different groups, each with its own purpose and structure. These are some of the groups that meet during the course of a week on the men's unit:

Community groups meet first every day and involve everyone on the unit. People get a chance to speak, or to read aloud something that is meaningful to them. Some of the material shared might come from a Twelve Step book or another source of positive affirmations. The group focuses on developing a sense of community and on solving their individual and collective problems. Each individual states his goal for the day, being clear about what he wants and defining how he will know when he has accomplished that task.

Process groups discuss what happens elsewhere in therapy. A group will process their experience on the obstacle course or talk about their reactions if a patient suddenly quits the program. The point of processing is to connect thoughts and feelings so as to clarify issues and reduce conflict.

Common Ground groups are unique because they are led by two therapists, one man and one woman. The focus is on helping men understand the ways women experience the world. During these groups men are free to ask the therapists anything they want to know: Why do women communicate differently? What is sex like for women? Obviously, no female therapist, no matter how well trained, can have all the answers. But the group gives men a chance to talk about things on their mind with a certified "expert" present. We do a lot of role-playing in these groups. At times the men will pretend to be women and thus experience firsthand what it is like to be sexually harassed or treated like an object. Such role reversal can be eye-opening for men who have never thought about what life is like for the opposite sex. Empathy for the other sex is key here.

Psychodrama is perhaps the most intensely powerful therapeutic experience in the program. Men act out emotional scenes that they want to explore and direct other patients to play various roles. For example, one man recreated a Thanksgiving dinner from his childhood, during which his drunken father threw the turkey through a window. The patient stood up and expressed the anger he felt toward his father, as he wished he could have done so many years before. Recently a man played out a scene in which as a boy he had to stand guard beside the family camper while his father had sex with the boy's older sister. After years of suppressing his pain, this man was at last able to cry. Another patient staged a moment when in a blind rage he had savagely beaten his 12-year-old son. Until then, he had been unable to forgive himself and had plunged into a suicidal depression. In the group, however, he replayed the scene, this time stopping short of actually hitting his "kid"—played by another patient—and instead asking his forgiveness. Through psychodrama, this man rewrote the script that had haunted him for months, and created a new and happier ending. This does not change the past but does impart a pattern of new behavior for the future.

Although psychodrama seems most dramatic and important to the person who creates and directs the scene, the audience often gets the most out of the experience. Observers see themselves in the drama that is acted out. At the same time they are able to think about what is happening.

After each group the men process what they have seen to

make sense of it and understand it. This debriefing is necessary to take the participants out of the past and back to the "here and now."

Family groups bring together one or more members from several of the patient's families. Having wives or parents or children present means they, too, can understand what is happening to the man. They can learn to be supportive of his treatment and discuss problems of their own. This group also offers an important opportunity for us to reach out to the women in our patients' lives. For example, if a wife objects to her husband wanting to have a "night out with the boys," we ask if she also objects when her son wants to spend time with his buddies. Usually, her answer is, "No, he needs to make good friends." We help her see that both of these men in her life have similar needs.

Perhaps a man isn't happy in his job but his wife presses him not to quit because they need the money. We ask the wife how she hopes her son's career will develop. She might say she wants him to pursue whatever makes him happy. We then help the woman see that the husband needs the same kind of acceptance and love she bestows unquestioningly on her son. In family groups the men and their family members learn to identify destructive patterns of family interactions and practice developing new behaviors for everyone.

Pyramid groups are devoted to personal problem-solving, especially learning how to handle power. In Pyramid groups, men learn when to hold on to power—and when to let go.

Men's Awareness groups discusses the way men are socialized. Subjects might include why men are made to feel disposable; why they don't live as long as women; relationships with fathers, and so on. Here men experience new options to free themselves from having to model their actions on the rigid role models they've experienced in the past. They explore new ways of being a father, husband, lover, or worker.

Wrap-up groups meet every night before bedtime and are another chance for people to express themselves in a community of men that offers a safe place to talk. They can go over what happened during the day, summarize their thoughts and feelings, and clear their minds before hitting the sack.

Goodbye groups meet when a man is about to leave the program. They offer a chance to say goodbye, to wish the man well, to express thoughts that may have been held back, to solidify a friendship. Each departing man takes with him a Goodbye Book containing names and addresses of the others in the unit, who may have inscribed a message, written a poem, or left behind a keepsake. Goodbye groups can be highly emotional. Recently an older man told a departing patient, "I'd be proud to have you as my son." Those were words the young man had never heard his father say, and he was overwhelmed. Another time, Sam, a 50-year-old man treated for alcoholism and depression, had become a true elder and a respected member of the group. As he left, the men said such things as, "Thanks for being the grandpa I never had." "You're the rock, you care." "You're a hell of an inspiration to all of us." "I never felt much like a man for the past forty-five years. You've helped me find out what being a man is really all about." The group stood and applauded as Sam walked from the room and out into the world, carrying with him a new understanding of his maleness.

OTHER ELEMENTS

Expressive therapy is physical in nature, compared to the talk therapy that takes place in other groups. This approach involves exercises to help men make the connection between their minds and their bodies. Another element is the experiential therapy described above, which in our facility is a structured program known as "Escape to Reality." This program poses physical problems for men to solve through cooperation and interaction: scaling twenty-foot walls with ropes, overcoming obstacles, and so on.

Art therapy works for some men because they find that through painting or working with clay they can express feelings more clearly than in words.

Occupational therapy (OT) teaches men alternatives they can use instead of falling back on the symptoms that brought them into treatment. One alcoholic patient, for example, learned how to make wallets. Afterward, when traveling on business, he always carried his leatherwork with him. When his business was finished, instead of heading for the hotel bar for a drink, he stayed in his room and kept his hands occupied. Busy work? In a way, but the "business" can be pretty serious: in this case, staying sober. OT also teaches men that they can do beautiful, intricate work with their hands and still be men, just like Roosevelt Grier, the former football player who does expert needlepoint.

Relaxation and stress management is essential, since men today are under enormous pressure. These workshops teach men how to recognize the "six D's" of stress: depression, defensiveness, disorganization, defiance, difficulties in making decisions, and an increase in dependency. Men then learn practical steps for reducing and coping with stress: visualization (a form of self-hypnosis), breathing exercises, meditation, and so on. Biofeedback is available to teach men how to gain some control over heart rate, breathing rate, even body temperature. Such strategies can help in controlling headaches, back pain, panic, and so on.

Workshops take place once a week and focus on different specific problems: how to stop smoking; how to negotiate with your wife about everything from sex to housework; understanding the differences in the ways men and women communicate, and so on.

Emerging Male Weekends, as we said earlier, offer the chance for a number of men to meet and grow together. While these events are not "therapy," in the strict sense of the word, they can be therapeutic. Through group discussion, ceremony, and ritual, men bond with one another and experience a degree of acceptance and love that they might never have known before.

ISSUES AND ANSWERS

Men come to therapy for different reasons. Once there, they find they share many of the same problems. Here are some themes that often crop up in our men's groups, and some of the ways we address them.

Anger: "When I got fired I was furious." "My wife didn't want to make love to me, and I got so pissed I kicked a hole in the door." Anger is usually the only emotion society allows men to have. Cry? No way. Rage? Go ahead, if you must. As a result men throw all of their other feelings—sadness, loneliness, fear—into a big pot labeled anger. In therapy men can learn to sort out their feelings and express them in appropriate and healthy ways.

Balance: "I don't let my emotions get in the way when I make important decisions." "I don't have to change diapers—that's her job." Men stress the physical and intellectual aspects of life at the expense of the emotional and spiritual ones. They may develop their male side and ignore their female traits—their ability to love, to feel, to nurture. In therapy they learn to develop a balance between the mind and the body, between emotions and logic, between gentleness and strength.

Bonding: "If I start telling some guy how I feel about him, he'll think I'm gay." Men fear getting close to one another. Or perhaps they just never learned how to share their feelings with another man, since emotional intimacy with a woman usually led to sexual intimacy. In men's groups they learn that feeling close to another man is not the same as sexual attraction; from that point, bonding—forming strong emotional ties—takes place with extraordinary speed.

Boundaries: "My mother always told me whenever my dad did something stupid or wrong. We kind of ganged up on him." Some men have a hard time defining who they are and what their relationship is to other people. The boundaries between people can slip, as when the father tries to make the son into a "pal." Sometimes the boundaries can be too strong, as in a family that refuses to allow the son to explore his world or play with other kids. Incest is the worst violation of boundaries, but there are many others. We teach men how to defend their boundaries and preserve themselves as whole individuals.

Common Core of Experience: "I sometimes think I'm the only one who's been through this kind of situation." In groups, men are surprised to realize that others share their feelings and their views. That helps to validate their experience, to make it both real and meaningful. For example, when asked who was the most important male role model in their lives, men often reply, "Coach." Others in the room nod their heads or mutter, "Yeah, coach." That single word is enough to tap into the men's common core of experience and help them bond closer together.

Communication: "My wife and I try to talk to each other, but it seems we're speaking totally different languages." There are differences in the way men and women use words, body language, and other tools of communication. Understanding that fact can help bridge the gap and lead to better relationships.

Competition: "If there's gonna be a winner, there's gotta be a loser." Maybe in sports, but not always in life. When a man feels he is "one-down," he is inclined to find someone else to stomp on so he can feel "one-up" again. In therapy he can learn that it isn't necessary to make someone else feel bad in order to feel good.

Control: "I'm the man—I'm supposed to be in charge." "If I let my wife push me around everyone will think I'm pussy-whipped." Control becomes a habit; men often are socialized to believe that they must direct not just their own lives, but those of everyone around them. Men need to see how surrendering control eases their burden but takes nothing away from their maleness.

Elders: "When I was growing up there were no men

around to show me the way." Today we tend to overlook a valuable natural resource: the older man, whose experience and wisdom have much to offer. In therapy we identify the elders, honor them, and listen to what they can tell us.

Fathers: "My dad was never there when I needed him." "My father didn't give me anything, so I give him nothing now." Men often have tremendous anger about their fathers. We teach men that they can understand why their fathers were the way they were. One man might need to learn that his father beat him because he was an alcoholic, not because the son was a bad person. Another might need to see that his father was absent, not because he hated his family, but because he had to work nights and weekends to keep them fed and clothed. Once they understand, they can then drop that burden of anger and get on with their lives. Men need to hear from other men that they are valuable, that they are worthy of care and respect. Men need, in other words, a blessing. They can learn how to turn to the community of men and ask for the blessing of the fathering that, for whatever reason, they never got.

Feelings: "Things just kept building up and building up until finally I exploded." Feelings are like gauges on a car dashboard that indicate something is happening inside. In therapy men can learn to read the information on those gauges. Equally important, they can learn that they have many choices in how they respond to a feeling. Anger, for example, need not mean they have to punch someone in the nose. Instead they might write a scathing letter to their Congressman or go work in the garden.

Grief: "When my father died I took care of the estate and handled all the arrangements. I was numb the whole time." "I felt like I changed when I was in Vietnam, like part of me died there." When we lose something—a loved one, a cherished relationship—it affects us the same as if we'd suffered a wound. We need to take time to understand we have been wounded and to absorb the loss. If we don't, the wound may never heal.

Intimacy: "I tell my wife everything about my work and about my hobbies, and she complains I'm not being intimate. What does she want?" Men can learn that for a woman, intimacy occurs face-to-face through emotional expression and emotional support. Men, in contrast, find that intimacy occurs side-by-side—riding in a car talking about politics, or watching the Super Bowl with the gang. We teach men that their definition of intimacy is valid, but that the women in their lives may be expecting something different. It's important to express intimacy both ways.

Isolation: "Sometimes I feel cut off from my family." "I don't get any pleasure from my work." By ignoring their own feelings, men sometimes fail to connect emotionally even with the people closest to them. When they are forced to carry out stereotyped roles, they may feel that there is no purpose to their lives. Therapy can help men end their isolation and help them connect, first with themselves, then with others.

Letting Go: "I have to wrestle with a problem until I've solved it, otherwise I'll be a failure." Men need to learn that when they've made every effort to solve a problem, and the problem still exists, the best thing may be to just walk away from it.

Mentors: "I knew what I wanted to be when I grew up, but there was no one to teach me." A mentor is a cross between a father, a teacher, and a friend, but doesn't carry their emotional luggage. A mentor embodies the qualities a man seeks and shows the man how to develop those qualities. If the mentor does his job right, the younger man eventually surpasses his teacher, at which point he no longer needs him. In our groups we teach men, first, the benefits of finding a mentor and, second, how to offer themselves as mentors to others.

Nurturing: "It's the mother's job to deal with the kids. Men are just supposed to provide and protect." We encourage men to understand and demonstrate that they are nurturing beings too. While their style of nurturing is different from women's, it is equally valid, but for different reasons. Women hold children close and keep them from pain; men take children to the canyon's edge and teach them to stand on the edge without fear. A mother may ask the young adult to stay at home forever; the father, lovingly but firmly, may know when it's time for him to go. Together mother and father teach the child how to leave home yet always be loved and connected to the family.

Personal Authority: "I spend a lot of time managing our investments to provide for my kids' future, but I feel guilty when my wife complains that I'm ignoring the family." We work with men to help them gain a solid sense of themselves. A man has personal authority when he makes decisions and stands by them without allowing others to shame him for his choices. It also means being strong enough to listen to others and change when the situation demands.

Power and Powerlessness: "I make the money, so I call the shots." "She thinks that because she's the mother, she's the one who decides how to discipline the kids." We teach men there are two types of power: the power of control, and the power of surrender. Both types are necessary for healthy living, and both must be kept in balance. Sometimes we need to control ourselves and others to keep ourselves safe, to grow and develop, to meet our needs. But sometimes we need to surrender—express our thoughts, share our feelings, ask for help. Surrendering is the essence of the Twelve Step approach, which urges people to turn their problem over to a Higher Power. True power lies in having the freedom to choose.

Responsibility: "I was so busy taking care of everybody else that I forgot to take care of myself." Society teaches men that they must be responsible. They must give up their dreams in order to provide for a family. They must make decisions—and suffer the consequences if those decisions turn out to be wrong. Men often assume responsibility for making other people happy and feel guilty if they fail. To give one example, men often feel that during intercourse they are personally responsible for making a woman achieve orgasm. In therapy men can learn that ultimately they have to become responsible for themselves. That means being responsible for their own feelings, and not assume that those feelings come from someone or something outside.

Roles: "I felt pressured to get married and settle down right out of college. I found myself with two kids and a career before I even knew who I was." We teach men that their roles are good, if they've chosen them, but they're not good if they were thrust upon them because of other people's expectations. We also show men that they should be flexible in their roles. As their circumstances change, they may need to adapt. If they feel they *have* to be the main breadwinner, for example, they may be in trouble when their wives start earning more than they do.

Role Models: "There was no one I felt I could look up to as a boy." "When I became an adult I had no idea what it meant to be a man." Many boys today are growing up in single-parent homes, without fathers, without older men to show them the ropes. Men forget that children notice what they do. We encourage men to conduct themselves in such a way that the younger men in their lives can emulate their behavior. We also encourage women to ask men—husbands, uncles, even neighbors—to remind them of their duty by asking them to serve as role models for their sons.

Self-esteem: "I get drunk so I can pass out and not have to look at myself in the mirror." Low self-esteem is a contributing factor in many psychiatric problems. Asked to write down twenty things they like about themselves, many men in treatment have trouble coming up with even three or four. In our program we honor the things about men that may have been overlooked—their experience, their insight, their special energy. We show men how to rediscover self-esteem by building on that solid foundation.

Success and Failure: "If I can't achieve everything I set out to do, I feel horrible." Men are in double jeopardy: They are under enormous pressure to succeed, and they suffer enormously if they fail. They think failure means they are personally inadequate. We work with men to show them how to separate feelings of failure from their feelings about themselves as human beings.

Work: "I took the job because the pay was great. I can't take the pressure any more, but I can't quit because everyone's depending on me." Many men believe that their work is their identity. They need to learn to separate who they are from what they do. One of our patients was perfectly happy driving a delivery truck for a snack-food company. He was promoted to manager, responsible for a whole fleet of drivers. He started working long hours, including weekends, but never felt caught up. Soon he developed depression complicated by panic attacks that in time prevented him from leaving the house. In treatment this man decided to give up his promotion for the sake of his health. His wife and even his parents were angry and made him feel he was passing up a "golden opportunity," but the men in his group understood his decision and supported him heartily.

GETTING BACK INTO THE GAME

The Men's Forum offers men a chance to retreat to a safe place for a while and nurse their wounds. Therapy is like a laboratory, where problems are broken down into parts and studied intently until the answers become clear. It's an artificial environment where men have the opportunity to meet others who share similar problems and who are also working on solutions. They can experiment with new behaviors, trying out feelings and testing their responses. If they make a mistake, it's okay—the other men can't fire them, disown them, or divorce them.

Eventually, though, patients have to return to the Real World. We try to prepare them for reentry as much as possible. Often it is necessary to schedule a special intensive week of family treatment attended by immediate family members. In some cases this means spouses and children; in other cases it means parents, brothers or sisters, or other family members. Back-to-work conferences with employers are often required to help both parties adjust to man's reentry into the world of work.

Another problem is preparing patients for the shock and disappointment they may feel when they realize that their families, friends, bosses, and neighbors probably won't understand what they've been through or how they've changed. Men graduating from the program have discovered how to deal with their feelings honestly and openly. They are eager to try out the new strategies they've learned. The other people in their lives, however, may not be prepared for that new level of honesty. That is one reason why family involvement and family therapy is so valuable during all phases of the treatment program.

To ease the transition, we encourage patients to take advantage of other programs to reinforce their changes and continue making progress. There is an alumni group made up of some of the hundreds of men who have graduated from the Men's Forum. There are ongoing support and therapy groups. Many patients continue regular attendance at Twelve Step programs. Frequently they join us for some of the Emerging Male Weekends. Some have even formed their own Men's Groups, meeting casually every two weeks or so in homes and churches.

In doing so they are part of a growing national trend, a trend offering hope that we can indeed save the males.

Chapter 12

OTHER PATHWAYS

In their search for a more fulfilling male identity, men today follow many paths. They are marching, sometimes literally, to a different drum. At this point the drum is still muffled, but the sound is growing louder.

Is there a Men's Movement? Better to say there are a number of men's movements, with a small "m" and the plural "s."

The trend began in the late 1960s and early 1970s, as a response to the changes women were making in their own lives. Redefining women's roles meant men had to adapt—whether they wanted to or not. By the mid-'80s a kind of men's network had evolved. Dozens of men's centers sprang up around the country. The National Organization for Changing Men began sponsoring annual conferences on men and masculinity. Some groups formed to demand political change—rights for gay men, rights for divorced fathers.

Today many groups promote personal growth and awareness. Some of these groups are quiet, taking place within a small circle of friends. Some are more visible, attracting media attention. Some, like our Men's Forum, address men's needs therapeutically. Some are led by professionals, others are self-run. All of these groups, however, seem generally headed in the same direction. They emphasize the need for men to rediscover their spiritual side. Men today seek an uprising—in the truest sense of the word.

THE "WILD MAN" MOVEMENT

A few years ago, public television ran a series of programs featuring Joseph Campbell, an expert on mythology. In interviews with Bill Moyers, Campbell showed how the ancient stories still resonate with meaning for us today.

Not long afterward, Moyers also interviewed the poet

Robert Bly. For more than ten years Bly has conducted workshops for men, helping them get in touch with their maleness. Bly uses poetry, myths, fairy tales, drumming, and other techniques to strike a chord within his listeners. His book on maleness, *Iron John*, stayed on the bestseller lists for months. Soon articles about the movement appeared in such publications as *The New York Times Magazine* and on television programs such as ABC's *20/20*.

The enormous exposure made people aware of a trend that had been growing for years. The polite, if awkward, name for the trend is the mythopoetic movement. More commonly, it is sometimes called the "Wild Man" movement. Interest in the movement is growing. There is even a publication called *Wingspan*, a quarterly newspaper with articles by and about men, that covers the movement from many angles.

The term "Wild Man" comes from a character in the Grimm's fairy tale, "Iron John." In his book and his talks, Bly retells this story of a boy's encounter with a hairy creature—the Wild Man—who carries the boy off into the woods. By the end the Wild Man has provided the boy with everything he needs to grow up and win the hand of a fair princess. As Bly interprets the tale, the Wild Man symbolizes the vital, primitive maleness that each boy must find within himself before he can become fully male and fully adult. The Wild Man is also a metaphor for the mentor that men need in their lives today but who is so often missing.

The workshops led by Bly and many others around the country often are part of a weekend of related activities—drumming, dancing, discussion. Depending on the leaders involved, there may also be programs in martial arts, meditation, environmental awareness, and so on. At some weekends, the men construct a Sweat Lodge, which one participant described as a kind of "sauna for the soul." Based on a tradition found in certain Native American cultures, the Sweat Lodge brings men close together, physically as well as spiritually.

The goal of the weekend is not to turn men into wild men, full of savagery and violence. Instead it is to help them understand that their "Wild Man"—a loaded term that simply means basic male energy—is a fundamental part of their being. Men need to respect and develop that part of themselves, just as they have to respect and develop their ability to be nurturers, lovers, and leaders. Bly himself says that trying to *be* the Wild Man, instead of just being *in touch with* him, ends in confusion and early death.

The Wild Man movement has confused and even alarmed

some people. On hearing that their men are heading off into the woods to dance and drum and sweat, many women think they have gone 'round the bend. Some hear the term "Wild Man" and think, "We have enough wildness in the world—what we need is a little more civilization." Others dismiss the whole thing as merely silly.

The confusion, while regrettable, is understandable. It arises partly from misleading and sometimes just plain bad publicity. Many reporters who have covered the weekends go there as observers, not as participants. (Far from being objective, some reporters are downright cynical, perhaps even embarrassed, about the whole thing.) They keep their emotional distance while watching dozens of men undergo a deeply spiritual transformation. They take pictures of men drumming and dancing, which is as futile as capturing the essence of a symphony or a ballet in Polaroid snapshots. The pictures and articles try to freeze moments that, for those taking part, are fluid and dynamic.

Of course, purely objective reports on Pentecostal church services or Hasidic rituals would also make them seem "silly" because such reports would fail to capture the drama and meaning of the events for those who are deeply involved. But society doesn't think of such events as silly, because we accept them as part of our broader culture. On the other hand, we have ignored equally significant influences from Native American, Asian, and African traditions. If nothing else, the Wild Man movement is helping us rediscover some of the lessons these cultures can teach us, just as we are rediscovering the deeper meaning of ancient folk tales.

OUT OF MANY, ONE

The tale of Iron John is just one story among hundreds that speak to men about their maleness. In our own reading, for example, we have found that the Biblical story of Jacob and Esau dramatizes the conflict between the wild and the tame sides of the personality. The legend of Parsifal, an Arthurian knight who sought the Holy Grail, reflects a struggle between the man's male and female inner forces. In the *Iliad*, the Greek epic about the Trojan War, Achilles wrestles with doubts about his ability to lead his troops and avenge the death of his beloved friend.

One reason such stories endure is that they express a basic truth. Men are complex beings. They have many parts. To become fully male, a man must develop each of his parts, achieve balance among them, and combine them into a unified whole.

The psychologist Carl Jung devoted much of his work to this concept. He believed that within each of us there is a primitive, collective unconscious that we have inherited from our jungle ancestors. That unconsciousness is expressed in the form of symbols, which he called *archetypes*. The archetypal symbols turn up in similar forms in myths and stories from all the world's different cultures. Examples of such symbols include the Hero, the Cross, the Flood, and the Mother. When we become consciously aware of these primitive symbols, they become powerful forces that guide our behavior.

Jung also believed that one's personality is the result of tension between pairs of opposite archetypes. For example, he stated that each of us contains characteristics of both the male (the *animus*) and the female (the *anima*). Another pair of opposites is extroversion (the urge to act, to relate to people and objects outside of oneself) and introversion (the urge to explore one's inner ideas and feelings).

Jung's ideas are more than just interesting theory. Therapists use his principles to help their patients find the less-developed parts of themselves. Men, for example, can recognize the feminine *anima* that exists within them and develop its intuitive, artistic aspects to enrich their lives. The goal is to achieve a balance in the influence of these opposites.

The Wild Man movement expands on many of Jung's ideas. The Wild Man himself is an archetype that symbolizes the vitality of our primitive drives. But there are many other archetypes, all competing for influence within our minds. Psychologist Robert Moore, working with mythologist Douglas Gillette, has given these archetypes names. The King, for example, represents our power of judgment and personal authority, our ability to define boundaries for ourselves. The Warrior has the job of protecting those boundaries. The Lover is the part that lets us dissolve boundaries so as to bond with something else. The Magician is a kind of teacher whose power to see beyond the "here and now" helps us understand the broader relationship among things.

A mature man is one who keeps these many forces in the proper relationship with each other. However, if the Warrior is too strong, the man will be overly aggressive. He will not be content merely to defend his boundaries; he will feel compelled to attack beyond them. If the Lover is dominant, then the man will be vulnerable; he may be controlled by other people's needs or his desire for experiences outside himself. A Magician that is too powerful may try to force his views on others, claiming special insight or wisdom.

As therapists, we feel that such ideas have practical value in dealing with our male patients. Symptoms of mental disorder can be seen as reflections of an imbalance among these archetypal forces.

For example, too much "King" causes a man to withdraw into his castle, refusing to share himself with others. Such a man may need help to express his emotions or to reduce his workaholic tendencies. A man with too much "Warrior" may need help dealing with rage and violence; if he has too little he will not stand up for himself, even when it is his right to do so. Too much "Lover" means he must learn how to reduce his dependency, whether on other people or on mood-altering drugs; too little means he can't make emotional connections and may need help for depression. An excess of "Magician" means the man needs to learn how to stop trying to control everyone and everything in his life, while too little means he may deny that there are real problems with which he must contend.

REDISCOVERING MALE ENERGY

How can men discover these archetypes within themselves? Once they've found them, how can they develop them to achieve the right balance?

At its core, the mythopoetic movement is an effort to rediscover these archetypes through the power of spirituality, a power that we in this technological age are in danger of losing. The key to spirituality is ritual.

A ritual can be any act that is performed with solemnity and ceremony. Calling something a ritual places a kind of frame around an event, a frame that says, "This is special, this has meaning beyond the action itself." A chef who carefully selects his utensils before setting to work is performing a ritual. So is the monk, for whom simply brushing his teeth represents an act of devotion to God.

In our work as therapists, we have found that rituals are a key to helping men tap into their feelings in a way that is comfortable, familiar, and safe. Rituals open the door to the unconscious, allowing us glimpses of the vitality stored there.

Rituals can be simple yet still be powerful. In the Men's Forum, for example, we give patients special T-shirts that we ask them to wear every Thursday. This ordinary gesture raises their awareness that they are part of a group, that the group has a serious and common purpose, and that their full participation is vital to everyone in the room. Similarly, in recovery programs such as AA, members recite the Twelve Steps, the Serenity Prayer, and other affirmations. When they speak they introduce themselves and are greeted by name. Such rituals put everyone on an equal footing and remind them of their common purpose in coming together.

A key ritual prominent in primitive cultures, one we have almost completely lost in our society, is initiation. The word means "a beginning." Boys today grow up without a firm sense of their transition into manhood. They don't know when boyhood ends and when manhood begins. For girls the situation is different. Many times the onset of menstruation serves as an initiation into adulthood. There are many ritualistic elements associated with this transition. The physical changes in the girl's body create a sense of anticipation. Often the girl's mother, older sisters, and friends become aware of the changes and prepare her for what is happening. There may be an air of secrecy and mystery about the process. Some schools send the boys out to play while the girls are shown a film about sexual maturity. The final event—the actual onset of menstruation—is clear-cut and well-recognized. As in many such rituals, there is even a sense of potential danger, since any loss of blood from the body can be frightening.

In our society, nothing so dramatic, clear-cut, or definitive happens to boys to indicate an important milestone has been passed. It's not surprising men are confused about their roles, about what society expects of them, because society doesn't bother to teach them. Boys are told they must be independent, that they will be measured by their achievements. But what's missing is a clear set of instructions spelling out their obligations to their community.

Initiations symbolize the death of the boy and his rebirth as a both a man and an adult. Typically, in primitive societies, the men drag the boy away from his mother and put him through some kind of ceremony that induces fear, if not actual pain. The elders also reveal the secrets of the tribe and teach him what he needs to know. Afterward he is welcomed as a man into the community of the tribe.

It is not the goal of a true initiation to create a test that some will pass and some will fail. Instead the goal is to help *all* the young begin their lives as adult males. That's where most of our modern versions of initiations fail. As writer Ray Raphael observes, "The task of a male initiation rite in any culture is to separate the men from the boys, but in our particular culture the practical effect of many of our so-called initiations is to separate the men from the men."

Fraternities stage initiations, but they of course exclude all those who are not members. Sports test strength and ability, but not all boys are athletic. Medical school, like the military, is a grueling process whose survivors join an elite group, but not everyone wants to be a doctor or a soldier. The bar mitzvah is a rite in which Jewish boys, on their thirteenth birthday, are welcomed into the community, before whom they declare, "Today I am a man!" The next day, however, they are back in school or back on the softball field. True manhood, with its many responsibilities, must wait a few more years.

One reason initiations work in primitive societies is that their members all share a common heritage. The number of members is also usually small. It's hard, in our melting-pot society with a quarter of a billion people, to find any common thread or tradition that unites all the people all the time. Because initiation is not interwoven into our social fabric, attempts at devising such rituals run the risk of creating spiritually empty imitations.

THE EMERGING MALE WEEKEND

We incorporate symbolic rituals into our therapeutic work with men. The opportunities for doing so in the hospital setting are limited. Resident patients have a full schedule of therapy sessions and other activities. They have a lot of intense psychiatric work to do during their typical four-week stay.

So, to expand our work with rituals, and to make them available to the larger community of men, we run a series of Emerging Male Weekends. The program has been influenced by our own positive experiences working with the leaders of the Wild Man weekends—Robert Bly, Robert Moore, Michael Meade, John Stokes, and others. While the Wild Man movement often encourages men to *explore* their wounds, our approach also encourages men to *heal* their wounds. Bly might ask his listeners to descend into their grief. We help them emerge from it. The weekends are not intended as therapy, but they are definitely therapeutic.

For many who come, such a gathering is the first time they have ever focused on the question of what it means to be a male. Never before have they spent time with men sharing stories, expressing feelings, and exploring common bonds. Intimacy, until now, meant shooting hoops or going fishing or drinking till all hours of the morning. For the first time, many of the men experience face-to-face intimacy.

The weekends may be held at a retreat, lodge, camp, or some other facility. Naturally, many men arrive with a sense of anxiety. They may have no idea what to expect, or they may have picked up a distorted impression of such events from newspapers or television. Some drive around for an hour or two, trying to decide whether or not to show up. We understand their anxiety and do our best to accept it and help them work through it.

Anywhere from ten to thirty men sign up for the weekend. Each is asked to bring a drum or other instrument. As soon as they arrive, sometimes even before a word is spoken, the drumming begins. The rhythm is spontaneous, hypnotic, resonating deep within their chests and drawing the men together. Such drumming may start spontaneously any number of times over the course of the weekend.

We then introduce the leaders of the weekend and describe our purpose in gathering. Any member of our clinic staff may take part, either as leaders or as participants—usually both. We may also bring in men with special skills, such as dancers or physical therapists, to conduct workshops in their areas of expertise.

THE GATHERING OF THE CLANS

As each man arrives we assign him to a smaller group, which we call a clan. Throughout the weekend the men will associate primarily with the others in their clan—eating together, talking together. That way they can get to know at least some of the participants better. During one recent weekend we set up four clans, each named after an animal. We suggested that over the next few days the men should think about the different types of male energy their animal represents. The Hawk clan, for example, might explore their soaring anger, while the Trout clan might explore the depths of their grief. (We first experienced clan activities at a week-long Robert Bly workshop.)

ACKNOWLEDGING THE ELDERS

Early in the proceedings we ask the oldest man in each group to identify himself. He becomes the Elder of the clan. It is not his job to have all the answers, but the others may turn to him if they need guidance or to settle a disagreement. Once, right at the start of a weekend, a man stated that he wanted to transfer from one clan to another, because he wanted to work on his anger, not his grief. Although they hadn't been together for ten minutes, the clan members instinctively asked their Elders for their thoughts. One Elder said if the man was unhappy, he was free to go; the other said if he wanted to join their clan, he would be welcome. Moments like this show clearly how the simple act of honoring men for the wisdom of their years gives them a power they never knew they had.

THE TALKING STICK

That first evening we conduct a ritual called the Talking Stick. (We've given a taste of that ritual in the prologues scattered throughout this book.) We explain that in certain Native American cultures, the men gather to discuss matters of importance. To ensure that each man who wishes to may speak—and to ensure that the others listen—they pass around a sacred stick. Only while a man holds the stick may he speak, and then he must say only what is in his heart. The others may not respond, except to say "ho" or "ah ho" if something the man says touches them emotionally. Following a short invocation in which we symbolically impart power to the stick, the ritual begins.

For many men, this may be the first time in their lives they have revealed their feelings in front of other men. Some men choose not to speak at first. By the end of the evening, though, having seen that the others will honor their right to be heard, they usually find they have something to say.

The stick is passed until no one wishes to speak any more. When the stick has made a complete circle without anyone saying anything, the ceremony is over. Sometimes a few times around is enough; other times the session may last long into the night. The stories that emerge during these solemn moments are astounding in the depth of pain and insight they reveal. In fact, we are beginning to incorporate the Talking Stick into our inpatient program, because giving such sessions ritual significance seems to stir men's emotions quickly and powerfully.

TALKING AND FEELING

The next day there is a full roster of events. Every weekend is different, with different goals and themes. This allows us to incorporate what we learn as time passes and to adjust our program to meet the needs of those taking part. What follows are some examples drawn from our recent Emerging Male weekends.

We may have a pre-breakfast exercise session. After the meal the leaders may tell stories—"Iron John" is a good one, but there are many others—that deal with issues of concern to men. The clans then assemble to discuss what meaning the story has for them. Following lunch we may do some activities that are more physical, such as trust exercises or group problem-solving challenges. We then ask the clans to get together and work out a presentation to give later during the campfire.

GRIEF AND INITIATION

One of the most important events of the weekend takes place that second night. After dinner the men assemble in the main room. We explain that we are going to stage a kind of initiation. We make it clear that such an event offers only a hint of what a true initiation, such as we described above, should be. Nonetheless our small-scale version may give the men a flavor of some of the emotions that they would feel in a "real" initiation.

First, however, we may do an exercise to explore our feelings. For example, in one exercise the men are asked to write down the three things they treasure most on separate pieces of paper. Deciding on just those three can be very difficult; the atmosphere in the room grows still. One man may choose his wife, his son, and his work; another may choose his life, his health, and his family. Often a man in recovery will include his Higher Power as one of his choices. Next we tell the men to close their eyes, select one of the papers, and throw it away. When the men realize what they have symbolically "lost," the feeling that comes over them is intense. A man who loses his son, for example, may regret that he never spent enough time with him. A man who loses his health may realize how much he has taken his body for granted. Through this simple exercise men focus on the positive things in their lives while experiencing grief in a safe but powerful—and temporary—way.

Often what follows is our own small-scale version of an

initiation ritual. We hand the men a sheet of paper on which is a question that we ask them to contemplate. One weekend the question was: "What have you done to prepare yourself to enter the Brotherhood of Men?" They think about their answer. Meanwhile, one by one, we invite each man to leave the others and come with us.

After a ceremonial cleansing—a ritualized washing of the hands—we lead him into a candlelit room. There, on a dais, sits the Elder of Elders wearing a ceremonial costume. The Elder poses the question and listens to the man's answer. If the answer appears to come from the heart, the Elder will confirm that the man has spoken well, and will tell him to go now and join the brotherhood of men. Each man is then guided toward a source of light—a campfire, where he is welcomed with an embrace from all those who have gone before him.

No words can convey the emotions that each man feels as he passes through the stages of this ceremony. To an outsider it probably sounds a little weird, perhaps downright corny; to those who take part, however, it is touching and beautiful. In contemplating the question, each man looks into his soul to find something that makes him feel worthy to claim the title of man. Then, alone in a dark room with a mysterious figure, he must give voice to his answer. The strange thing is, he *knows* he is play-acting; he *knows* the man behind the mask is one of the weekend leaders. *Yet something reverberates deep inside him, telling him this is a moment like no other.* When the Elder accepts his answer, the man—for perhaps the first time in his life—accepts himself. Then, beside the campfire, he is given acceptance by dozens of others. He has truly entered the Brotherhood of Men.

After this experience, things lighten up. Each clan gives its presentation—a skit, a personal revelation, perhaps a dance. We end the evening with laughter, songs, and conversation. The fire dies away, but the good feeling continues to glow for a long time afterward.

The next day we discuss the events of the night before. We remind them our exercise was in no way a true initiation. Nonetheless the feelings they experienced were very real and very important. One man said he felt so good after leaving the presence of the Elder that he wasn't sure if he ran or flew to join the campfire. Another said he felt a sense of rage—"Who the hell has the right to tell me whether I've been 'accepted' or not?" Both feelings are valid. Most men, however, report experiencing a totally new feeling. As one man remarked, "I finally realize that I have what it takes to be a man. I *do* deserve to join the Brotherhood."

We break into clans one last time to allow the members a chance to say goodbye to each other. We might ask each man to present an object he has found that symbolizes his experience during the weekend. Recently one man displayed a pine cone, saying that, like the cone, this gathering was a collection of many separate parts that came together to form a cohesive whole. Now the time has come to break apart, but in doing so the seeds will scatter, grow, and continue to spread the good feeling. Another man held up a thorn, saying, "I know I can be a pain in the ass, but I really enjoyed spending time with you guys." After a final Talking Stick ceremony (and a pause for a group picture), the weekend comes to a close.

THE AFTERMATH

Do men's gatherings produce any long-lasting effects? Do the feelings generated in a Wild Man weekend or an Emerging Male weekend last beyond the time the men are together? In our experience, the answer is yes.

One "alum" called us to report that he had formed a group with some of the guys he had met during the weekend. They were getting together every other week just to talk and share what was happening in their lives. Another man said the weekend had reminded him of the value of male companionship, and that he was now doing a lot more talking on the phone and visiting with his old buddies. Some men make it a point to attend two or three men's weekends a year. One told us his experience had reactivated his feelings of love for nature, and that he had started camping with his family again for the first time in over ten years. He said he especially enjoyed serving as a "nature mentor" for his two boys. Another man, an attorney, started writing poetry again, a hobby he had abandoned as he developed his career.

ARE WE GOING IN THE RIGHT DIRECTION?

A tribe of aborigines in Australia, now extinct, had carried out a ritual for over eight thousand years. At key points in the ritual it was the leader's job to stop and ask: "Are we going in the right direction?"

In our efforts to save the males, we too need to pause once in a while and consider the same question. So far, the signs are very encouraging.

Men today are taking a close look at the roles society has scripted for them. Sometimes they agree that, yes, these are the roles men should play. Other times they demand a rewrite. As therapists, we make it our job to help them redefine who they are and what they want to be.

Men are changing as women change. They realize that greater equality for women can work to their own advantage. Just as women demand flexibility in their roles, so too can men. They need not be the sole provider for their families—*if that's what they choose*. They can change careers in midlife to follow their truest dreams—*if that's what they choose*. Before, masculinity meant rigidity and firmness. For the new man, masculinity can mean flexibility and change.

One thing that will probably remain constant is the way men derive much of their identity from their work. Businesses are slowly realizing that they must adapt to the changing needs of men and their families. Flexible work schedules, split shifts, paternity leave, time off to handle family crises— all of these will contribute enormously to men's sense of well-being. The process of change has only barely begun. As men continue to gather together and share their stories, however, their voices will grow louder and the change will occur more quickly. Men are becoming pro-active.

Men are also learning how to be flexible in their roles at home. For some time now society has encouraged men to be more sensitive and involved as fathers. Women who have demanded that men do their share of the chores are realizing that painting the house, fixing the gutters, and taking care of the yard count toward fulfilling that obligation. Some couples have worked out a type of arrangement we may be seeing more in the future: He works in the morning while she takes care of the kids, then they switch jobs for the afternoon. Or he works one year while she stays home, then the next year they reverse. Such couples are usually self-employed or have untraditional jobs that allow them the luxury of such flexibility. It is likely that in the future small businesses may recognize the value in offering such benefits to their workers. Part of our clinic's community outreach involves educating executives about the special needs of their male employees.

The popularity of the mythopoetic movement and other facets of the men's movement are other signs that we are moving in the right direction. Through myths and legends, men are discovering the deeply rooted drives that shape their feelings and behaviors. Understanding the male archetypes means men can develop those parts of themselves that they have suppressed or ignored. Ideally, as the writer Mark Gerzon observes, we will even create new archetypes to enhance those we already have. As the Persian Gulf war revealed so vividly, the Warrior today has access to weapons of awesome precision and destructiveness. There comes a time when the Warrior, his task finished, must yield to a new archetype, the Mediator. The Mediator believes not in winners and losers but in the value of mutually beneficial solutions. Other archetypes for the New Age are the Healer, the Colleague, the Companion, the Nurturer. Men are complex; there is room inside them for all of these images of masculinity.

One of the most encouraging indications of progress is the growing willingness of men to help other men. Groups are forming in living rooms, in office cafeterias, in churches and community halls to focus on issues of masculinity. They are creating a new kind of male intimacy. They are learning the importance of serving as mentors to the young. Their success encourages other groups to form and grow.

How will we know when males have been saved? We will know because they are men who extend their hands in friendship, not in anger; who do not rape, but revere; who honor women, the planet, and themselves with the blessing of their masculine energy.

When we meet such men, we will know instinctively that they are going in the right direction. We can also trust them to point out the path, so that others may follow.

Epilogue

A Ring Around the Moon

During one of our recent Emerging Male weekends, we witnessed a bit of magic.

We had just completed our initiation ritual. Each of nearly three dozen men had looked inside himself to find an answer to the question posed by the Elder of Elders. Each had been found worthy to join the Brotherhood of Men.

We all assembled, warmed and welcomed, at the fire. Linking arms around each other's shoulders, forming a circle with the fire blazing in the center, we sang a quiet song.

A burning log collapsed and sent a burst of sparks skyward. We looked up.

A near-full moon shone overhead. And there, completely circling the moon, was a ring of pure light.

Our circle of men, ringing the fire, found its reflection in the mirror of the moon.

The sky looked down on us and gave its blessing.

Men's Resources

Publications

Man!: Men's Issues, Relationships
  & Recovery
Austin Men's Center
1611 West Sixth Street
Austin, TX 78703
(414) 477-9595

Men's Studies Review
P.O. Box 32
Harriman, TN 37748
(615) 369-3442

Men Talk
3255 South Hennepin
  Avenue, Suite #45
Minneapolis, MN 55408
(612) 822-5892

The Talking Stick: A
  Newsletter About Men
182 Thomas Jefferson Drive,
  #200
Frederick, MD 21701
(301) 829-2460

Wingspan—Journal of the
  Male Spirit
Box 1491
Manchester, MA 01944
(Wingspan contains listings of
  men's activities throughout
  the country, as well as many
  local and regional men's
  centers.)

Bibliographies

Men's Studies
Eugene August
Libraries Unlimited
P.O. Box 263
Littleton, CO 80160
($30)

Men's Studies and Issues
  Reading List
Gordon Clay
National Men's Resource
  Center
P.O. Box 882-WS
San Anselmo, CA 94960
(Free; send stamped self-
addressed envelope)

Organizations

American Psychiatric
  Association
Division of Public Affairs
1400 K Street, N.W.
Washington, DC 20005

Help for Problems

General

National Self-Help
  Clearinghouse
33 West 42nd Street
New York, NY 10036

Alcoholism and Addiction

Alcoholics Anonymous
World Service Office
P.O. Box 459
New York, NY 10017

Alcohol and Drug Abuse
  Problems Association of
  America, Inc.
444 North Capitol Street,
  N.W., Suite 181
Washington, DC 20001
(202) 737-3430

Alcohol, Drug Abuse, and Mental
  Health Administration
5600 Fishers Lane
Rockville, MD 20857
(301) 443-3783

American Medical Society on
  Alcoholism and Other
  Drug Dependencies
6525 West North Avenue, 204
Oak Park, IL 60302
(312) 848-6050

National Clearinghouse for
  Alcohol and Drug Information
P.O. Box 2345
Rockville, MD 20852
(301) 468-2600

National Council on
  Alcoholism, Inc.
12 West 21st Street
New York, NY 10010
(212) 206-6770

National Federation of Parents
  for Drug-Free Youth
8730 George Avenue, Suite 200
Silver Spring, MD 20910
1-800-554-KIDS

National Institute on Alcohol
  Abuse and Alcoholism
5600 Fishers Lane, Room
  16-105
Rockville, MD 20857
(301) 443-6480

Depression

National Alliance for the
  Mentally Ill
1901 N. Fort Myer Drive,
  Suite 500
Arlington, VA 22209-1604
(703) 524-7600

National Committee of Youth
  Suicide Prevention
666 Fifth Avenue, 13th Floor
New York, NY 10103
(212) 957-9292

National Depressive and
  Manic Depressive
  Association
Merchandise Mart, Box 3395
Chicago, IL 60654
(312) 939-2442

National Institute of Mental
  Health
Public Information Branch
5600 Fishers Lane
Rockville, MD 20857
(301) 443-4536

National Mental Health
  Association
1021 Prince Street
Alexandria, VA 22314
(703) 684-7722

Post-Traumatic Stress Disorder

National Association of
  Veterans Administration
  Chiefs of Psychiatry
54th Street and 46th Avenue
Minneapolis, MN 55417
(612) 725-6767

U.S. Veterans Administration
Mental Health and
  Behavioral Sciences
  Services
810 Vermont Avenue, N.W.,
  Room 915
Washington, DC 20410
(202) 389-3416

U.S. Veterans Administration
Readjustment Counseling
  Service (10B/RC)
810 Vermont Avenue, N.W.
Washington, DC 20410
(202) 233-3317

SOURCES

Acker, Kathy, "Manpower," *New Statesman and Society*, 2: 52 (June 2, 1989), p. 12.
American Psychiatric Association, *APA Journalist's Reference Set*. Washington, D.C.: American Psychiatric Association, 1988, 1989.
American Psychiatric Association, *Diagnostic and Statistical Manual of Mental Disorders, Third Edition, Revised*. Washington, D.C.: American Psychiatric Association, 1987.
American Public Health Administration, "Position Paper on Men's Health Problems Policy (1985)," *Men's Studies Review*, 7:4 (Fall 1990), p. 8.
Angier, Natalie, "A Potent Peptide Prompts an Urge to Cuddle," *New York Times*, January 22, 1991, pp. C1, C10.
Bly, Robert, *Iron John: A Book About Men*. New York: Addison-Wesley, 1990.
Butts, Dan, and Michael Whitty, "Men's Health and New Work Values," *Men's Studies Review*, 7:4 (Fall 1990), pp. 9–17.
Clayman, Charles B., and Jeffrey R. M. Kunz, eds., *Men: How to Understand Your Symptoms*. New York: The American Medical Association/Random House, 1986.
The Diagram Group, *Man's Body: An Owner's Manual*. New York: Bantam Books, 1977.
Durden-Smith, Jo, and Diane deSimone, *Sex and the Brain*. New York: Arbor House, 1983.
Ehrenreich, Barbara, *The Hearts of Men: American Dreams and the Flight from Commitment*. Garden City, N.Y.: Anchor Press/Doubleday, 1983.
Farrell, Warren, *Why Men Are The Way They Are*. New York: Berkley Books, 1988.
Fennel, Reginald, "Contemporary Issues in Men's Health for College Males," *Men's Studies Review* 7:4 (Fall 1990), pp. 18–20.
Filene, Peter G., *Him/Her/Self*. Baltimore: The Johns Hopkins University Press, 1986.
Gayle, Jacob A., "Introducing Men's Health: A Special Issue," *Men's Studies Review*, 7:4 (Fall 1990), p. 3.
Gelman, David, "Fixing the 'Between,'" *Newsweek*, July 2, 1990, pp. 42–43.
Gerzon, Mark, *A Choice of Heroes: The Changing Faces of American Manhood*. Boston: Houghton Mifflin Company, 1982.
Gould, Mark A., *A Consumer's Guide to Psychiatric Diagnosis*. Summit, N.J.: The PIA Press, 1989.
Halper, Jan, *Quiet Desperation: The Truth About Successful Men*. New York: Warner Books, 1988.
Hightower, Newton A., "Working With Rageful and Violent Patients in Group Psychotherapy," *Houston Group Psychotherapy Journal*, 3:1 (March 1989), pp. 15–33.

Jovanovic, Lois, and Genell J. Subak-Sharpe, *Hormones: The Woman's Answerbook*. New York: Fawcett Columbine, 1987.

Kimmel, Michael S., "Of Mice and Men," *The Nation*, July 10, 1989, p. 63–66.

Korin, Daniel E., "We Are Our Brothers Keeper, Changing From Within or Creating Critical Consciousness in Health Delivery: Applications of Freire's Philosophy and Methods in Providing Health Services for Men," *Men's Studies Review*, 7:4 (Fall 1990), pp. 1, 3–7.

Lawlor, Robert, *Earth Honoring: The New Male Sexuality*. Rochester, VT.: Park Street Press, 1989.

Levinson, Daniel J., *The Seasons of a Man's Life*. New York: Alfred A. Knopf, 1978.

Lieberman, Alexis, "Why Men Are Afraid of Doctors," *Prevention*, February 1988, 91–95.

Liebchen, M.P., "War Underground: Tunnel Rats in Vietnam," *Veterans of Foreign Wars of the United States Magazine*, 78:5 (January 1991), pp. 32–34, 38.

Martin, Ellen James, "Work Gone Awry," *The Bergen Record* (Hackensack, N.J.), January 14, 1991, p. C1–C2.

Moore, Robert, and Douglas Gillette, *King, Warrior, Magician, Lover: Rediscovering the Archetypes of the Mature Masculine*. New York: Harper & Row, 1990.

Moreines, Robert N., and Patricia L. McGuire, *Light Up Your Blues: Understanding and Overcoming Seasonal Affective Disorders*. Summit, N.J.: The PIA Press, 1989.

Morris, Stephen R., "Strong, Silent and Suffering," *Newsweek*, April 3, 1989, pp. 10–11.

Pruett, Kyle D., *The Nurturing Father*. New York: Warner Books, 1988.

Raphael, Ray, *The Men From the Boys: Rites of Passage in Male America*. Lincoln, Neb.: University of Nebraska Press, 1988.

Reinisch, June M., and Ruth Beasley, *The Kinsey Institute New Report on Sex*. New York: St. Martin's Press, 1990.

Sabo, Donald, "Denial and Men's Responses to Illness and Death: Critical Feminist Perspectives," *Men's Studies Review*, 7:4 (Fall 1990), pp. 23–27.

Slaby, Andrew E., *Aftershock: Surviving the Delayed Effects of Trauma, Crisis and Loss*. New York: Villard Books, 1989.

Spence, Janet T., and Robert L. Helmreich, *Masculinity & Femininity: Their Psychological Dimensions, Correlates, and Antecedents*. Austin, Tex.: University of Texas Press, 1978.

Stearns, Peter N., *Be a Man! Males in Modern Society*. New York: Holmes & Meier Publishers, 1979.

"Study Finds Severe Effects From Childhood Abuse," *New York Times*, February 18, 1991, p. 11.

Styron, William, *Darkness Visible: A Memoir of Madness*. New York: Random House, 1990.

Swanson, J.M., and K.A. Forrest, *Men's Reproductive Health*. New York: Springer Publishing Co., 1984.

Tiger, Lionel, *Men in Groups*. New York: Vintage, 1970.

INDEX

A

Abuse of males, 104-118
  causes, 105, 108
  as children, 106-108
  physical, 105
  sexual, 105-112
  by women, 109-112
Achievement, obsession with, 21, 22
Addictions, 67-78
  to work, 112-114
Aggression, male, 24, 33, 35
Alcohol abuse, 5, 43, 55, 68, 97
Anger, 25, 56, 92-103
  appropriate expression of, 94-95
  identifying trigger for, 102
  images of, 98-99
  as issue in therapy, 100-103, 140
  myths about, 98
  problems related to, 95-98
  social sanctioning of, 93
  as symptom, 97-98
Anorexia, 116, 117
Antidepressants, 58-59, 86
Archetypes, 17, 150-151, 159-160
Art therapy, 139

B

Balance, issues of, 140
Barker, Art, 8-9
Baywood Hospital (Houston, Texas), 3, 8, 10, 131, 132, 133
Behavioral therapy, 136
Beliefs, reprogramming, 135
Bly, Robert, 14, 24, 35, 37, 53, 94, 100, 129, 130, 148, 153, 154
Bonding, male, 3, 48, 140-141
Boundaries, as issue in therapy, 141
Brain, and gender-related functional differences, 43-45
Bulimia, 116-117

C

Campbell, Joseph, 14, 147
Ceremonies. *See* Initiation ceremonies; Rites of passage; Rituals
Children
  abuse of, 106-108
  nurturing of, 25-26
Chromosomes, 41-43, 46
Clans, 154, 156
Cocaine, 74-76, 97. *See also* Drug abuse
Cognitive therapy, 135
Commitment, flight from, 34
Common Ground groups, 137
Communication, gender differences in, 141. *See also* Talk, male
Community groups, 136
Competition, 21, 22, 35-36
Conduct disorder, 96-97
Control
  emphasis on, 21
  as issue in therapy, 141
  male stereotype of, 20
  of rage, 99-100, 102-103

D

Denial, 11, 126-127
  of alcoholism, 70-71
Depression, psychological, 53-66, 84
  eating disorders and, 116
  psychotherapeutic approaches to, 58-66
  symptoms of, 55-57
  types of, 53-54
Deviant behaviors, 47
"Disposable male," 8, 11-12
Divorce, 114-116
Drug abuse, 55, 67-72, 74-78, 97

E

Eating disorders, 116-117

Ehrenreich, Barbara, 32, 33, 34
Elders, 157
　acknowledging, 154-155
　as resource, 141-142
Emerging Male Weekends, 3-6, 8, 11, 15, 51-52, 121-122, 140, 146, 153-154
　described, 153-158
　initiation ritual, 161
　lasting effects of, 158
　participants, 3, 133
Emotions, 156
　communication of, 124-125
　father's lack of guidance about, 29
　as issue in therapy, 142
　restriction of, 21-22, 24, 36, 54-55, 93
　talking about, 14
Energy, male, 133, 148, 151-153
Environment, of gender-specific therapy group, 87
Epinephrine, 45
Expectations, of society, 18-21, 32. *See also* Gender role(s) *headings*
Experiential therapy, 136
Expressive therapy, 139

F
Failure, handling, 11, 145
Family groups, 138, 145-146
Farrell, Warren, 8, 16, 25, 29
Father(s)
　demands of being, 10
　as issue in therapy, 142
　as male role models, 13, 28-28, 37
　son's relationship with, 10, 13-14
Feelings. *See* Emotions
Feminine attributes, of males, 23-24
Feminine Mystique, The (Friedan), 33
Filene, Peter, 48
Film/television images of manhood, 14, 28-29
Freud, Sigmund, 13-14, 123
Friedan, Betty, 33

G
Gathering of Men, A (program), 3
Gender identification, 18
Gender role(s), of men, 18-19, 27-28
　educating men about, 134-135
　effect of divorce on, 114-115
　hazards of, 21
　as issue in therapy, 144
　need for freedom of choice in, 19, 35-38
　reevaluation of, 159
　symptoms in relation to, 53-118, 130
　scripts of, 134
Gender role(s), of women, 124
Gender role strain, 21-23, 28
Genetics, 27, 41-43
Gerzon, Mark, 160
Gillette, Douglas, 150
Goodbye ceremony, 158
Goodbye groups, 138-139
Grief, 142, 156

H
Healer archetype, 160
Health, 21, 22-23
　men's special needs regarding, 129-130
　smoking and, 72
　stress and, 45, 113
Heredity, 41-43
Homophobia, 21, 22
Homosexuality, 111
Hormones, 46-48
Husbands, 10
　abuse of, 109-110

I
Incest, 106-108, 141
Initiation ceremonies, 152-153, 156-157
Intermittent explosive disease, 97
Intimacy, 10, 29, 142, 154, 160
Iron John (Bly), 53, 94, 148, 156
Isolation, as issue in therapy, 143

J
Jung, Carl G., 14, 17, 150

K
King archetype, 17, 150

L
Learning disabilities, 117-118
Letting go, as therapy issue, 143
Levinson, Daniel J., 130
Logical thinking, 24, 44
Longevity, 11-12
Lover archetype, 17, 150, 151

M
McCaughtry, F. Rex, 9
Magician archetype, 17, 151
Maleness/masculinity
　archetypes of, 150-151
　attitudes toward, 12-13, 33-34
　attributes of, 23-24

Maleness/masculinity (cont'd)
  in gender-specific group therapy, 87
  tales of, 148, 149
  Wild Man as symbol of, 148
Manic depression, 53
Marijuana, 75, 97
Marriage, 34, 114, 115-116
Meade, Michael, 153
Men Treating Men (program, Baywood Clinic, Houston), 133
Men's Awareness groups, 138
Men's Forum (program, Baywood Clinic, Houston), 8, 9, 10, 136, 139-146, 147
  alumni groups, 146
  approaches used in, 139-140
  issues addressed in, 140-146
  types of groups used, 136-139
Men's movements, 147
Mentors, 143, 148, 160
Midlife crises, 130
Moore, Robert, 17, 150, 153
Moyers, Bill, 147
Mythopoetic movement, 148-161

N
National Organization for Changing Men, 147
Native American cultures, 148, 149, 155
Nurturing, 25-26, 143, 160
Nurturing Male, The (Pruitt), 25

O
Obesity, 116
Occupational therapy, 139
Options, importance of, 37
Oxytocin, 47-48

P
Persian Gulf War, 34-35, 80, 160
Personality disorders, 96
Post-traumatic stress disorder (PTSD), 79-91
Power/powerlessness, 11, 21, 22, 143-144
Process groups, 136-137
Pruitt, Kyle, 25
Psychiatry. *See* Psychotherapy *headings*
Psychodrama, 137
Psychoeducational approach, 134-135
Psychotherapy
  approaches to, 59
  traditional, 9, 14, 126-128, 129
  women and, 123-124

Psychotherapy programs for men, gender-specific, 3-6, 7-8, 10-11, 15-17, 19, 131, 132-161. *See also* Emerging Male Weekends
  approach of, 10, 15-17
  for depression, 59-66
  goal of, 15, 130, 134
  issues dealt with in, 140-146
  most important aspect of, 86-87
  men treating men in, 131, 135
  for post-traumatic stress disorder, 85-91, 86
  problems responding to, 10-11
  therapeutic strategies used in, 134-136
  versus therapy with mixed groups, 125-126
  types of groups, 136-139
  value of, 125-126
  women in, 16
Pyramid groups, 138

R
Rage, 11, 93-94, 96, 99-100, 102-103
Rape, 94
Raphael, Ray, 152-153
Relaxation techniques, 139-140
Resistance to treatment, 126-128
Responsibility, as therapy issue, 144
Rites of passage, 130-131. *See also* Initiation ceremonies; Rituals
Rituals, 3, 4-6, 130-131, 151-153, 155, 158. *See also* Talking Stick ritual
Role(s), male, 18-19, 27-28. *See* Gender role(s), male
Role models, male, 13-14, 28-29, 144

S
Scripts, of roles, 134
Seasonal Affective Disorder (SAD), 53-54
Seasons of a Man's Life, The (Levinson), 130
Self-esteem, 56, 116-117, 127, 144-145
Sex
  versus gender, 18
  genetic differences, 41-43
  as weapon, 94
Sexual behavior, restrictive, 21, 22
Sexual drive, 46
Shame, 9, 56
Smoking, 72-74
Socialization of males, 18-21
  historical view, 30-35
  need for new script for, 35-38
  power of, 27-38

Stereotypes
  of men, 18-26, 44, 134
  of women, 114
Stokes, John, 153
Stress, 45, 113-114, 139-140
Substance abuse, 67-78, 85. *See also* Alcohol abuse; Drug abuse; Smoking
Success issues, 21, 22, 145
Suicide, 53, 56, 57
Symbols, archetypal, 150
Symptoms
  archetypal forces and, 151
  of depression, 55-57
  and gender-roles, 53-118, 130

T

Talk, male, 16, 128-129, 156
Talking Stick ritual, 4, 155
Testosterone, 46
Thinking, disturbed, 57
Tiger, Lionel, 30, 48
Tobacco, 72-74
Treatment programs for men. *See* Psychotherapy programs for men, gender-specific

V

Veterans. *See* Post-traumatic stress disorder; Vietnam conflict

Vietnam conflict, 33, 34, 79-80
Violence, 94, 97-98
Visualization, 135, 140

W

War, 5, 24, 31-32, 33, 34-35, 160. *See also* Post-traumatic stress disorder
Warrior archetype, 150, 151, 160
Warrior Training (treatment program), 3
Wetcher, Kenneth, 8
Wetcher Clinic (Houston, Texas), 3, 8, 10, 131, 132, 133
Why Men Are the Way They Are (Farrell), 16
Wild Man archetype, 17, 150
Wild Man movement, 3, 17, 147-149, 150, 153
Wingspan (journal), 148, 149
Wolfe, Tom, 34
Women
  men's relationships with, 10, 16, 35, 109-110, 112
  traditional psychiatry and, 123-124
Women's movement, 19, 33, 123, 130
Work, 11, 25, 37, 112-114, 145
Workshops, 140
World War I, 31-32
Wrap-up groups, 138